Good Girl Bad Girl
My Father's Daughter

My Journey an Open Book

Revelation 12:1

Janene Prudler

ISBN: 978-0-692-86587-3

Recharge Ministries Publishing Company
New Mexico

Chapter illustrations by Coy Prudler (author's grandson)
Book design and layout by Lighthouse24

Contents

Foreword .... *v*

Acknowledgments .... *vii*

Introduction 1

1. Fatherless 3

2. I Want My Daddy 10

3. House Not a Home 17

4. My Defying Personality
   Don't You Touch Them 24

5. Left Alone Unprotected 33

6. Myasthenia Gravis
   Was This the Last Night of my Life? 38

7. The Unrelenting Fight for My Life 46

8. Addicted to Alcohol 54

9. Out of Control 62

   Pictures 69

10. He Loves Me He Loves Me Not
    Searching for Love in all the Wrong Places ... 76

11. What Was I Hooked To?
    Was This My Future Husband? 87

12. Bottomless Pit of Self-destruction 96

13. Journey from Rebellion to Surrender 104

14. My Three Miracles
    A Step of Faith against the Unknown 111

15. Redemptive Lives
    Freedom into the Light 119

16. No Longer a Broken Vessel 128

17. He Who is Forgiven Much Loves the Most 130

18. Memories of the Father's Love 137

19. He's Calling Your Name 143

20. Pearl of Great Price 149

21. A Reflection of My Father's Love 154

    In Closing 155

Foreword

When asked to write a forward for my longtime friend Janene, I was more than willing and very much honored. She is a mighty woman of God who has touched my life deeply. We have known each other for over thirty years, five and a half of those living in close proximity to one another. Therefore I can say we really got to know each other during that time.

In the early years I participated in a weekly women's Bible study held in her home in Hanson, Massachusetts. I clearly remember sitting on the floor at her feet listening intently to every word she spoke. I guess you could say I looked up to her. I still look up to her because she continues to look up to the Lord in all she does.

Janene is a woman who I call a spiritual bulldog because when God calls her to do something, she sinks her teeth into it and doesn't let go until the thing asked of her is done. I have witnessed this many times. This book is the product of her determination and devotion to God to do just that.

Through the process of writing this book many days, weeks, months and years have been spent in deep prayer and soul searching to bring to fruition all God has asked of her. She has opened the pages of her life for all to see; the good, the bad and even the ugly.

Throughout most of her life Janene did not receive love from her earthly father. You will be amazed at all that happens before she feels that love and so much more. Her search had been as they say, "In all the wrong places."

Janene's prayer is to see other captives set free from all that held her captive for too many years. God loved her more than any man or woman could. What He did for her, He can and will do for you if you surrender it all to Him.

Pasty Darmetko

Acknowledgments

Under no circumstances do I believe that any Christian book written or published could be of value without acknowledging first and foremost the leading of the Holy Spirit. As I was approaching the closing of this manuscript, I found it most difficult to reveal my name as the author of *Good Girl Bad Girl, My Father's Daughter*. I prayed and entreated the Holy Spirit's help knowing that in and of myself I had nothing to write which could change anyone's life. I will be forever grateful for the Holy Spirit's wisdom in helping me fulfill this assignment the Father gave me.

It would be remiss of me to not recognize those who have helped make this book ready for publication. I greatly appreciate their encouragement which resulted in my being able to keep focused on this assignment. I want to thank the following people: My husband Robert, daughters Leah, Jessica, and my good friend Pasty who spent hours reading through each chapter for editing. My three sisters Betty, Janet and Kaylynn who encouraged me to write my story. Published author Ron Lewis for his support and prayers, Author Richard Evans for his expertise in Microsoft Word, and a special thanks to the team at Lighthouse24 who helped make this book acceptable for printing.

A special thanks to my grandson Coy Prudler who drew illustrations to highlight some of the chapter titles.

Introduction

Wonderfully and Fearfully Made!
How was I to believe that?

AM I SOMEONE'S DAUGHTER? Whose? When I wanted to be the Heavenly Father's daughter, I could not! Life for me presented many struggles in my search for a love that cannot be described in human terms. I knew it existed, but I couldn't seem to accept that I was worthy enough to receive it. I had felt such rejection from my own father and stepfather and it made me feel as though there was something wrong with me.

Was I so unlovable? When you read my story you will understand why I would question the Father's ability to love me. I knew when I became a Christian Jesus loved me, but how was I to identify with God as my Father and me as His daughter. You will understand my battle for acceptance by the time you finish reading this book.

When I considered that some of what I am about to reveal in this book could possibly offend a loved one, I began to struggle with this question, *"Is this really what you asked me to do Father?"* I didn't give much thought at the time to the implications this would have on me or others who had been involved in my life if I were to accept this assignment.

To respond in obedience would require me to trust that His purpose was more powerful than any adverse effect it might have on me. I would be exposing portions of my life I would normally not share with many people. My willingness to disclose what I would rather remain hidden comes from my desire to please the Father.

I wish I could share with you that I had this amazing revelation of the Father's love for me at the time of my salvation. I did not! How could I understand and accept the Father's love when I felt no love from my earthly father as a child growing up. It would take many years for me to believe and accept the unconditional love of the Father. For this reason I want to bring to light through my testimony how the Father will never abandon His attempt to convince you of His love. It's important that we never give up the search for such an amazing love that surpasses anything that a human father could ever hope to give us.

My intention is not to give credit to the enemy by exploiting the details of my past, but instead show the height, depth, width and length that my Heavenly Father went to for me, His daughter. Every voice that yelled, *"You are unworthy"* was completely silenced by His love.

It's with such love and gratitude that as I looked back on the details of my life I was able to identify the times the Father was present and not willing to let me go. Through some of the saddest days of my life, a disease that nearly took my life at the young age of seventeen, to the countless moments of loneliness I felt, He was always watching over me. I pray that through the writing of this book you will experience a renewed hope that will allow you to embrace the Father's love and desire for you.

You will see this symbol ♥ placed throughout the chapters indicating the places where I believe the Father was drawing me to Himself when I had no awareness of it at the time. Each one of these ♥ represent the many pieces of a puzzle that make up my life. I do believe the final piece concerning our lives on earth will be when we take our last breath before being ushered into His presence.

Fatherless

Dear Dad,

Until I was asked to write this book I thought all the emotions I once felt about you as my father were in the past. Instead, I find myself living parts of my childhood all over again as I recall much of what life was like growing up. I had hoped to detach myself from any emotions that might surface as I started this chapter on feeling fatherless. Instead, it's as though I'm a little girl again remembering what it was like having you absent for much of my life. They say you can't turn back the clock, but it feels like that is exactly what I am being asked to do.

So much of how I handled life and the decisions I made came from my sense of unworthiness. I grew up believing if I was not important enough for my own father to be more involved in my life there had to be something wrong with me. How else was I to interpret my worth if most of my childhood seemed like a continuous feeling of rejection? You walked away from our family for a woman you thought was more important than us. I was your little girl and needed you, but you had other plans. I know it's too late to change what can never be, but I wish you could have understood how very much I needed to know you loved me.

My childhood love for you as my father left me blind to the truth. I finally came to understand the gravity of my situation when I was old enough to feel this deep yearning in my heart that went unfulfilled. It was never going to happen for me the way other little girls dreamed it would be with their fathers. I lost out on more than you walking me down the aisle. They say that little girls look to their dads as their first love and male role model. I had neither! I was robbed of your love and all the valuable lessons fathers can teach their daughters.

I am not writing this chapter to point out all the mistakes I thought you made. I came to understand that we all stand guilty of making wrong choices that can affect the ones we love. Though I have been forgiven of the things I am ashamed of in my past, I recognize my need to share and withhold nothing in order that others might have the opportunity to experience the healing and forgiveness I have received. There are many like myself who were very much affected by painful circumstances that occurred in their lives. If those reading this book can identify with their own need for healing, it is my hope that they will allow the Heavenly Father to bring healing to the scars of their past as He did for me.

In closing my letter to you, I wanted to express my disappointment in your lack of response to the notes I wrote to you before you died. I was concerned, Dad, that as you were nearing death you were ready to meet your creator. You were my father and I wanted to know where you would spend eternity. I tried to reach out to one of your daughters to learn more of what your relationship with the Lord was like over the years. I received no response from her. I still hold onto the hope that you are safe in the arms of Jesus.

Your daughter, Janene

P.S. My final visit with you was the hardest rejection I have ever felt as your daughter. I am glad that you are no longer here to read the end of this chapter. It would not be my desire for you to be reminded of what you are no longer able to change.

My Life without a Father

It isn't easy for me to write about my life and allow not only my family but others to see a side of me most have never known. I hardly know where to begin to reveal what I would rather remain hidden. In no way could I have imagined that while writing my biography I would be faced with portions of my life I had never considered before. It forced me to confront truths that were painful and yet brought to light how much the Father protected and loved me even though I was unaware of His presence. It took years to allow the Lord to break down this enormous brick wall in my life. I had no ability on my own to remove the effects of abandonment, betrayal, intimidation, molestation, and a life of addiction to both men and alcohol.

When life doesn't turn out the way you imagine, you start to reflect on where things started to go wrong. Having accepted an assignment to write my biography has challenged me to look back at what I first remember as a child. It is a picture that if given a choice, I would decline to remember. Perhaps it has remained a part of my life for the sole purpose of writing this book.

When I reflect on my earliest memory it leads me to consider whether or not my birth was something my parents had planned for. At the time I was conceived, good Catholics such as my mother were not allowed to practice birth control. This obligation to the church ultimately resulted in many unplanned children being born. Though I will never know for certain if my birth was intended, what I'm aware of now is this; I was in fact a part of God's plan. My initial reason for questioning my parents desire to have another child was due to the events of that fateful night my father showed up with another woman.

Little children often wake up during the night scared and find themselves crawling into their parent's bed. I suppose I qualified for that privilege being the youngest of three children. That's exactly where I was on the night my life was about to change forever. Clearly visible from the bedroom stood my father with another woman in our living room. Though I observed the entire scene, I was too young to know what it meant. I was three years old, a time when children live to give and receive love. We learn through our parents the word yes and no. We are gaining an understanding of what is good and what is bad. I didn't have the propensity at that age to discern what this would mean for my future. What we do have as children is the ability to see images and to remember what we saw.

I would learn later I wasn't the only one watching what was taking place in our home. My older brother also woke up and saw what was happening. Frightened and too young to do anything, we both stood helpless and watched. What we saw taking place that night is still alive in our memories today. Though I don't recall the words that were spoken, I know it would not have made a difference. What mom did next clearly communicated how she felt about what she witnessed in our living room.

I remember watching mom jump out of bed and head straight for the bathroom. The bathroom was to the left of the bedroom, but not visible from the bed. I was not about to be left alone so I did what any little child would do and followed my mom. Even as I write about this episode it feels like I am standing there beside her in the bathroom. I recall how bright the light was above us as though it had no cover. That's when both my brother and I remember mom grabbing for a hairbrush. Odd as it may seem, I have never forgotten the details of that image.

It was evident that my mother intended to go after my father. In retrospect, I can't imagine what was in her mind as to what could be accomplished with a hairbrush. Though I don't recall much of what happened after she grabbed the hairbrush, what I do know now is this; that was the night this little girl became fatherless. The meaning of abandonment would not be a word I could possibly understand at such a young age. In the years to come it would be all too clear just what it meant.

From what I was told my father occasionally would show up where we lived. Mom allowed him to come knocking and she would leave the door open. Some of us can identify with what it's like to experience such a sense of loneliness that we allow things into our lives that are not healthy. Mom found herself in a situation where she was not strong enough to say no to my father though he was obviously still the same person who walked in that night with another woman. Mom was left to deal with the reality she was still in love with the one who also vowed "until death do us part." It has to be hard to love someone who does not love you back enough to want to fix the marriage. In the future, I would know all too well what that would feel like.

My father was gifted with very good looks and those external qualities kept him searching for new excitement. It was hard for women to resist his good looks and a smile that would capture their attention. Though he left our family to marry another woman, it was only the beginning of the trail of devastation he left behind. Many more of his children would be left without a father's involvement in their lives.

I can appreciate that my father finally settled down and stayed with his last wife for many years. They had a beautiful daughter who was blessed to have him throughout her life until he passed away. He also had stepchildren he was very much a father to. From what I have seen and heard, he loved them as much as they did him.

I understood from his absence in my life just how blessed they were to have him in theirs. What I share in the following pages about my father is not to discredit him as a person. It's important for me to detail the emotions and basic needs that children have, so it might have the potential to awaken fathers and mothers to be active in their children's lives no matter what path they have chosen.

There were many times throughout the years I wondered if my father truly loved me. We could all be asked to write the definition of love and most of us would define it differently. Love to me is seen by the actions of the one who says they love you. I cannot speak for my other siblings and how they felt about their father being absent while they were growing up. It is heart breaking for me to realize at times how I am still very much affected emotionally when I recall so much of my life without a father. In the past, pain and tears began to surface when I was reminded I was not worthy enough to be a part of his life. I find myself choking up when I look into the face of rejection as I recall my past. I believe one of the reasons I am writing this book is to let go of any of the residual effects I have experienced as the result of my father's absence in my life. Only then can the Lord complete the healing process He started in me.

The more I write the more I am able to see how much we are all guilty of making bad decisions. My Dad was like many of us who have followed the leading of our own desires without thought of the consequences to others. I find myself having to look within at the many mistakes I have made in my own life. If it were not for my Redeemer, where would I be today?

I find it easier for me to write the details of my childhood before I reached an age where the emptiness of not having my father in my life became a reality. Now that I am starting to evoke memories of my life at the age of six, I feel this strong need to type with my eyes closed. I'm not happy about what I am feeling. Do I really want to travel back to the many times there was a need for my daddy, yet my daddy was not around. Who would keep me safe from those who could hurt me and would hurt me?

Recalling this portion of my childhood is still painful for me and there is nothing I can do to change it. I could walk away right now and decide it's too much of a price to pay to be reminded of what never was. Because so many of us have scars in our lives that need healing, I must press on and write my story for their sakes.

My parent's eventually divorced and mom later met a man whom she married after knowing him for only three months. Whether she married for love or out of necessity, it would not have made a difference in the end. Mom did what she felt she had to do. Most of us can understand her need to seek help raising three small children. There was no way mom could have known what the good times or the bad times would look like in this marriage. There would be both!

My birth father agreed to allow my mother and us children to move from Michigan to Arizona with her new husband as long as he didn't have to pay child support. I assume that seemed agreeable to him as he would be relieved of his responsibility to care for us. My real anger became intense when I look back and realize that my father walked away from us without taking the time to make sure he was placing his children in the hands of a good man. Not even our mother foresaw what our future stepfather was capable of.

Would our life be miserable? Was this man who became our stepfather void of any trace of goodness in his heart?

—2—
I Want My Daddy

EVEN IN THE MOST DIFFICULT TIMES when growing up it didn't register in my heart that my birth father was unavailable. When I was being mistreated at home, my first response would be, "I want my daddy!" Those were the very words I used many times when I found myself in trouble. I would go to my bedroom and cover my head so as not to be heard. I was so intimidated growing up with my stepfather that I lived to avoid being his next victim.

Summers for me would prove to be a short escape from reality. I'm not sure if I looked forward to summers as a way to be closer to my birth father or to be out of harm's way for a few months. Either way I longed for the time when school vacation rolled around. Mom would make plans for us to travel to Michigan to be with family. I went to one set of aunts and uncles while my siblings went to stay with other family members. Though I would be two thousand miles away from my mother, I knew I would be nearer to where my father lived. What little girl wouldn't be filled with the anticipation of being with her father whom she hadn't seen for ten months?

My summers for the most part were filled with wonderful memories of time spent with aunts, uncles, cousins, and grandparents. Their homes provided unconditional love and a place where we felt wanted. Though we were given the opportunity to be with family, the one person missing that I longed for was my father. There was no way for me to let go of this longing in my heart day after day as I waited for him to come for me. I waited and I waited, but he never came. How could he be living so close and yet so much of the time be unavailable? I would have been excited if I could just hear his voice on the phone. Perhaps he did call once or twice, but it certainly isn't something fixed in my memory.

It's not that I am without fond memories of being with my dad. There were times that he would take us to the lake to swim. While we swam he would be laying on his blanket covered in baby oil tanning his body. Most of what I remember when I was with dad involved an outing that interested him. When I look back over my summers in Michigan I wonder if dad just spent time with me out of necessity.

I enjoyed the few times we would sit around a campfire near the lake while he played his guitar and sang. One song I remember he loved to play was, "Listen to the Rhythm of the Falling Rain." I had the opportunity to download the album recently and realized the power music has over our lives. Every song on the album encouraged the lifestyle my father went on to lead. Hearing that song today has always placed me at the campfire with my father. He always seemed to have a smile on his face and seemed happy playing his guitar and singing.

Storybook endings don't always come to fruition just because we want them to. The most painful memory that remained with me for years took place the evening I arrived at my father's cabin. I was not sure who drove us to see our father that summer night, nor do I remember how old I was. I was so excited to see my dad I could hardly wait for the car to stop before I opened the door and jumped out. I was heading straight for the cabin when I spotted him and his third wife Nora through the window. I thought to myself, "I'm going to surprise him!" I knocked on the window knowing he would be so happy to see me, or so I thought!

I'm not certain what my father felt that night. Looking back I have always concluded the joke was on me! I'm grateful I was too young to think it was anything but excitement on his part to see me. Nevertheless, it was a picture that held me captive well into my adult life. I eventually was able to see the writing on the wall. My very last visit with my father confirmed what I came to understand, childish dreams don't always come true and life can be harsh at times.

Dad had others in his life that he would need to divide his time with. Circumstances altered his ability to keep our family together when he was building another family at the same time. It wasn't his decision that we move two thousand miles away. Though he allowed my mom to leave, it would only make it harder for us and him. I know it sounds callous to say, but in all reality, out of sight and out of mind made it easier for him to deal emotionally with us not being in his life. Dad would have to work harder if he wanted to be a father to us. In the end that proved to be too difficult for him. Many of his other children grew up without him in their lives as I did.

My father was human with an unredeemed nature like all of us are before we come to Christ. We often find ourselves making mistakes that others pay the price for. By the time dad married for the third time he had already walked away from seven children who needed him. I was only one of his children who would bare the emotional scars of not having him actively involved throughout their life. I believe as a father he could have impacted all of our lives in a positive way if circumstances would have been different. The choice is always ours to make when it comes to what we do with our life.

Somehow through all of this writing, I understand there is a self-seeking side to all of us. My father made the choice to live the life he did and in the process he could not have possibly met all of the needs of his offspring. If there was any desire to pursue a relationship with him the effort had to be made by me. I still cared about my dad and had not yet given up on having his involvement in my life. I would have to find a way to meet that need on my own if I wanted to be a vital part of his life. I was losing hope as time went on that he might desire a relationship with me. I was now a married women with children of my own and knew it was time to let go of wanting something that seemed impossible. My time of making failed attempts came to an end.

It all happened one evening while some of our families were in Michigan visiting my brother. My father who lived near my brother invited us to come over one evening. The invitation included my sister and her husband, myself and my husband. Though my mother and stepfather were visiting my brother at the time with us, the invite certainly didn't include them. Understandably so! When it was time for everyone to leave I made the decision I would not be going. In my heart I had done enough fooling myself and was simply finished making the effort. It seemed a lot to ask of myself to refuse the invitation, but I knew it was the right decision to make. Dad could not change who he was and it wasn't fair for me to determine what was in his heart that evening. It did not prevent me from continuing to care about him. It would be close to nine years before I paid him what turned out to be my last visit.

I received a call from my brother that my father had congestive heart failure. I can't be certain how much time we were given to make arrangements if we wanted to make the trip to see him. If I recall, it was not something we had to decide that day and yet a decision needed to be made fairly soon. My sisters and I decided we would purchase plane tickets and meet in Michigan. It took some serious praying on my part about making the trip as I felt there was not much left of our father daughter relationship. He was still my father and I was still his daughter regardless of how I wanted to interpret that. I was no longer angry with him, nor did I have an overwhelming need to see him. So much time had passed, I had already prepared myself for, "what is, is!"

It came time to respond to the call my brother made concerning my father's failing health. It was not out of a sense of love that compelled me to make this last visit to my dad. I felt as a Christian it would not be a good witness to our relatives if I chose not to go, so I purchased a ticket and made arrangements to meet my sisters.

I was able to forgive my dad because I was able to face my own sinful nature and knew what I had been forgiven of. I made many wrong decisions during the years where alcohol ruled my life. I hurt the ones I loved through my selfish actions.

What I was not prepared for was my father's lack of response toward me in our final time together. There was no evidence of his love whatsoever for me as I sat on the couch with my sisters that day. At the time I was not sure that I was expecting a positive response from him; however, when our visit ended it was another opportunity for me to experience his rejection. I did not come prepared that day for what actually occurred. I traveled two-thousand miles and paid for a ticket I could hardly afford. He barely acknowledged my presence the entire time I spent in his living room that day. I left knowing what I have always known. For anyone to say my dad loved me would have been an absolute affront to what my heart knew to be the truth.

I will always be thankful my older sister was there that day to witness the truth of what I had just experienced, or should I say what I did not experience! I suppose in the end I still needed some sign I meant something to him, but there was no hint of love, just death to any remnant of hope I had, death to his love and death to everything I wanted as his daughter yet would never have.

I take full responsibility for the bad choices I have made in the past which you will read about in the following pages. I'm not laying blame for my choice entirely on my father. What I am saying is this; my sense of feeling unloved and without value started as a result of the night my father chose another woman over us. I pictured my life that night as a set of dominos being stood up ready for a chain reaction to knock them down. My father's decision to be involved with another woman started the first domino falling in my life. When the first domino was touched, the rest of the dominos would continue to fall until something or someone stopped them. Those dominoes would not stop falling until the Heavenly Father's hand reached out and changed my life. It wasn't something that happened overnight. There would be many dominos falling before I came to the place where I nearly destroyed my life.

Much of the wrong decisions I made were a by-product of how I saw myself. When my father surrendered his responsibility to care, nurture, love, and support me as his daughter it left a deep wound in my life. How could I believe I had worth if my own father walked away from me so easily? I would continue my search for significance well into my young adult life. It would take years for the wounds of rejection to play themselves out. Much of my childhood was a reminder to me of who I was and who I was not in the eyes of those who were supposed to love me. It led me on a path of self-destruction until thankfully the Lord intervened.

Earlier in this chapter I talked about how love is shown by our actions. I have come to understand through writing this book that I did love my father. If I had not, I would have given up making any effort to seek out his approval and love. I held onto such hope well into my adulthood. Living so far from each other discouraged any attempt to try and form a father-daughter relationship.

When I fell as a child and hurt myself I had no father to run to comfort me. Though my outward scar remains visible today to those who look, it cannot be compared to the internal scar that needed healing in my life. I write and share my story so you can find help to forgive those wrongs done against you. I trust you will understand your Heavenly Father can heal the scars of your past. I hope as you read this book you are able to grasp the immeasurable love and length the Father will go to in order to bring you to Himself. You can be certain what He has done for me, He also wants to do for you. You will find that the wounds of your past become the very circumstances the Lord will use to touch and change not only your life but the lives of others.

There are some in my family who might be troubled by my decision to write a book about my experiences as a child growing up without my father. I can accept that each of my father's children may have a different sense of how their lives were affected growing up; however, this is my story and how I saw my life and my experiences with my father.

If I chose to suppress the truth in order to protect myself or to protect others from getting hurt, who am I really hurting in the end? Some will choose to go on believing that everything was perfect, but nothing ever is. In the chapter titled, "Redemptive Lives" you will understand more of why I chose to risk writing this book and especially this chapter.

Writing did not prepare me for facing my own failures as a mom. Through this entire chapter I have looked at my father's failures and realized I am really seeing my own. My story of feeling unloved does not end here!

Some of you reading this may feel convicted by your past and can identify with the mistakes my dad made as well as the ones I made which you will read about. This book is not meant to bring condemnation on what cannot be changed, but to help us understand what a forgiving Father we have. If He can bring you or I through a life meant to destroy us, we can freely embrace Him as our Heavenly Father. It is my hope that some who read this book will understand that the decisions you may make in the future can have dire consequences on yourselves or on others.

I'm grateful that God has accomplished much of the healing that needed to be done in my life and He will continue to do as I write this book.

—3—
House Not a Home

I HAD THE OPPORTUNITY to have two men as fathers that could have made a difference in the way I dealt with life and the choices I made. While I was a child, neither of them demonstrated any kind of love or nurturing. I went from being abandoned by my father, to being placed in the hands of another man to raise me. A man whose unredeemed nature filled my heart with fear as I grew up. I spent twelve years in a house with a stepfather reacting to whatever his flesh demanded.

I remember so little about my childhood until my mother remarried. Had I known I would be writing today about this portion of my life in a book to be published, I would have sat down with mother and sought answers to many of the questions that have eluded me. The difficulty in starting to write this chapter is feeling as though my life is depicted like a scene in *Star Trek* where I am beamed up from one scene and placed in the next scene with very limited knowledge in between. It started from the night I woke up to see my father standing in the living room with another woman until I was being raised by a man who was anything but loving while I was growing up.

I am somewhat unsettled as I start this portion of my story. Though it may be hard to understand the truth is, until now, I have never felt the need to dredge up my childhood experiences and question why my mother married a man who abused her children. I'm not sure if I should be experiencing anger or accept there is a higher purpose in retelling guarded details meant to be kept in secret.

When you forgive someone that has reconciled their life with the Lord, you see things differently. I can look back over the years and feel nothing but love for the man my stepfather became in the last years of his life. Some reading this chapter may not understand my choice to love a man who found pleasure in abusing me and my siblings. For me to withhold and minimize who this man was before his transformation would limit your ability to see what the Father is capable of doing in each of our lives.

When I was six-years old my mother remarried. I will always believe she would never knowingly choose a man who would spend years making life difficult for her children. The cruelty and mistreatment I received from his hands had nothing to do with me not being his biological child. Ernie had three children from his first wife who also experienced unspeakable occurrences in their home. Who this man was continued to be manifested from one family to his next. We were his next family.

I'm feeling an overwhelming need to understand what led my mother to marry someone she had only known such a short time. If I took time to reflect on the years mom was single and the challenges she encountered, it would better help me understand and accept some of the choices she made; choices that had damaging consequences for her children. I felt certain where I needed to start looking.

My mother woke up one night and stared into the face of my father who was standing in our living room with another woman. It would take time for the shock of what she just witnessed to pass before she could understand what this would mean for her and her three small children in the days ahead. One day she was living in a home with a complete family and the next her family was fragmented. She had no husband and we had no father. She would face struggles for the next three years that she could never have anticipated. I'm starting to gain a better understanding of what might have led her to make a hasty decision in her choice of a husband and a father for us.

My birth father no longer showed any interest in seeing that his children were being cared for or supported. The weight of what my mother was expected to carry went beyond her financial burdens. It takes both parents to adequately provide for the care and needs of their children. She found this to be true when she faced one of her biggest challenges during the time she was on her own.

Though I fully understand the man my birth father was, I still find it difficult to believe he was so callous in how he responded to my mother's need for help. Suffering with a ruptured appendix and too sick to drive herself to the hospital she reached out to my father for help. She not only asked for a ride to the hospital but needed him to watch us children. It would only seem reasonable for him to step in with compassion to help her. Not so! My mother's plea was met with his pre-occupied self-indulgence. He dropped her off at the hospital and left. Alone and suffering, she said she prayed for death.

My father did the unthinkable because he sought what pleased him regardless of who he hurt in the process. Mom had lost the husband she loved to another woman. Lying in a hospital bed with nothing to look at but the ceiling she succumbed to the weight of what she was facing. The loneliness and fear she experienced brought her to a point of exhaustion. She became despondent and ready to give up on life. It was during that time that a priest walked into her hospital room to visit. She shared with him that she no longer wanted to live. His admonition to her was, *"No, you have every reason to live. You have three beautiful children who need you."*

I can only imagine how difficult life must have been for mom during the years she was without any help raising us. Overwhelmed with responsibilities, she perhaps came to a weak moment in her life where she thought giving up was the only path forward.

I believe it's possible for any of us to reach a crisis in life when our world seems to have fallen in. Turbulent times happen and if there isn't anyone to encourage us, despair sets in and we began to lose hope. I believe her feeling of hopelessness looked like an insurmountable mountain to overcome. Her need for help certainly could have played a part in her making the decision to marry someone she hardly knew. A man whose actions and behavior proved to be detrimental to the well-being of her children at times.

If I chose to leave out the problems my mother faced when she was struggling to take care of us, you might never understand the decisions she made to marry someone she only thought she knew. For years we faced the side of a man who could not restrain his anger. In such a short time there was no way for our mother to know what this marriage would mean for her children. I suspect that by the time you finish reading this chapter you may ask yourself the same question I did. How could a mother stay married to a man who continually mistreated her children?

There seems to be no need for me to go into more details of what life was like for mom in the years she was single. Most single moms struggle to keep their families together while working and making the time to meet the needs of their children. Mom was no different except she did it without the help that is available to many single moms today. She loved her three small children she called her stair steps and did whatever she needed to in order to provide for them. Mom reached a point of needing help and help presented itself while she was working the assembly line at the Ford Motor Company in Detroit, Michigan.

While focused on what she was doing at work, she was approached by a gentleman who stopped to ask her for directions.

Though she said she never looked up at him she later admitted it was the voice of this man, Ernie, she was first attracted to. He thought she was cute and was determined to make some inquiries about her situation. It wasn't long before he asked mom out and extended the invitation to bring her three children. From what I was told it was only a few months later they decided to get married.

Mom was the picture of many young women today who decide to remarry to make life for themselves and their children easier. I will never be certain if that was the deciding factor in her marriage to Ernie. Many who find themselves in similar circumstances often choose someone they know so little about. My mother did exactly that. Three months was not enough time for her to know what was behind the voice she was so attracted to. There is an African proverb that says, "Wherever a man goes to dwell, his character goes with him." I am certain Ernie did not reveal his true character or his past behavior during their courtship. The words that were communicated during those three months that convinced my mother he was a man worthy of marrying, held little truth. It was later that his true character would overpower who he portrayed himself to be. Ernie was controlling and intimidating with an incredible demanding character that came to dwell in our house.

Mom may have thought she knew the man she was marrying after three months. It would take her children less time than that to dislike him. I remember one day my sister and I were standing up against the corner of Ernie's house near his fenced-in back yard. My sister was nine at the time and I was three years younger than her. While looking at his dogs inside the fence, I heard my sister say, *"I wish his dogs would eat him!"* I was not sure at the time what elicited that kind of response, but I knew life as a new family for us was not starting out very well. When I reflect on the words she spoke that day I think to myself, "Wow, what strong emotional words coming from someone so young." I can only assume that she had already encountered his anger at some point. Surely, something happened to trigger those emotions. When I recently asked if she remembered saying those exact words she said, "No!"

I found myself stopping here to question why some people remember certain situations while others forget. Having spent much of my life recalling negative events made me want to search out the "how come" aspect of this scenario. I knew where we were standing that evening and I'm able to recall the exact words she spoke. I've since come to understand that our brain has a tendency to register and remember negative experiences and retain them more than positive ones. Though we all process emotions differently, it seems we are more likely to reflect on the unpleasant events and may use stronger words to describe them. If I have ever wondered before why I was able to recall so much of the hurtful things that took place in my life with such detail and clarity, I now have a better understanding.

It's possible that evening we were either hiding from Ernie or did not want him hearing anything we said. I understand that my sister had a difficult time with the idea of another man in mom's life. If Ernie put his hand on top of moms she would pick it up and remove it. I can easily surmise this didn't sit well with him. Most of us can understand a child becoming resentful of someone trying to take the place of another parent. She was so young and even though our birth father was not often around, he was still her father.

It does not surprise me that children sometimes have a better perception of people than adults. My sister will tell you the first night Ernie showed up at our door for a date with our mom, she knew she wasn't going to like him. I don't believe she ever outgrew her dislike and would later come to hate him with reason. You would have to know my sister to understand how her love of her Savior gave her the ability to finally release her anger and pain to the only one who could bring the healing she needed.

Words from my older sister: *"In the last years of Ernie's life, he asked me for forgiveness. Because I did not live in the same state, it was easier for me to see that he suffered with guilt. I hated him, yet loved him in the end because he found Jesus."*

You would think that our new stepfather coming into our lives would make every effort to present a loving impression on his stepchildren. I don't remember Ernie displaying much love and affection towards us when we were little. Who he had been to his first family before us was precisely how he treated us. One does not change abusive behavior simply by changing families. One's true character will manifest itself if there is not an internal transformation. For Ernie, that transformation would take years for any of us to see.

—3—
My Defying Personality
Don't You Touch Them

MY LIFE WAS ABOUT TO CHANGE and I had no idea what those changes would look like. Abandonment has distinct ability to leave internal scars that manifest themselves in our actions and in the way we perceive ourselves. On the other hand, physical abuse often times will leave a different set of scars that become especially noticeable in future relationships. I experienced a great deal of both of these situations I needed to somehow overcome. I could never have done this on my own and it would take the hand of God and many years to repair the damage that resulted from much of my childhood.

Though my mother endured her husband's many moments of rage, she was determined to make the best of her situation. It would be her children who would ultimately pay the price for his often sadistic desires. Having not been given a choice to have this man in our life left us no alternative but to submit to his authority.

Though it is painful to recount past abuses, some of my sisters have consented to allow me to share some of their story as they experienced it. We understood that there would be no way to show others the remarkable change that occurred in Ernie's life if we left out who he was before he met his creator. I'm able to write about the man I once hated and later learned to love.

When I knew I would be writing this book, I needed to take into consideration there would be other family members who stood a chance of being hurt if I chose to be honest and open about my childhood. I first sent off an e-mail to my stepsister. If I was going to be writing about her birth father I wanted her to know the reason I felt it was important to share my story. In my writings, I would be bringing to light just who their father was when he came to be our stepfather. I needed to explain why I was willing to tell the truth as I saw it. She was a beautiful Christian woman and I respected her enough and wanted to make her aware of what I felt called to do.

The miles that separated us limited the times we saw each other over the years. They were older and their visits never prompted a discussion about what their home life was like growing up. I don't believe they would have felt comfortable discussing any part of their childhood while Ernie was still alive. Until I started to write this book there had never been any mention about what life was like for them. When I received an e-mail response back and read what she had shared with me, I was taken aback. If my mother had known what took place in their home with their father while growing up I believe she would have refused his advances and turned down his proposal.

Her willingness to allow me to share her response in this book has given me the opportunity to write a more accurate description of who this man was for many years as our stepfather. If I chose to discard the contents of this letter you would never have the opportunity later to read how God brought about the remarkable changes in her father's life.

Words from Ernie's biological daughter:

Dear Janene,

I'm so sorry that I did not respond to this e-mail right away. I also felt unloved as a child. My parents had a bad marriage. They were the babies in their families and spoiled. There was constant fighting and drinking. I thought they were the most selfish people that I knew. I remember many a time when they would come home from the bar and they would be quarreling. Dad would want to know where my sister hid the gun because he wanted to kill my mom. He then proceeded to beat her. My sister and I would wait up for them to see how they were. My poor sister! She had so much responsibility that I thought of her as a mother. I would go to her for advice instead of my mom. They divorced when I was thirteen years old.

I turned my back on God during my teen years. I didn't feel that He could love me as I was, so I tried to earn His favor by doing good works. When I failed to be good enough; I quit trying. I did not understand Grace.

I have no illusions about how my dad was when he married your mother. He beat us kids and I am sure he beat you and your siblings.

The changes that took place in her father's life can be read in the chapter titled, "Redemptive Lives."

God brought my sister through a childhood that was defined by anger, violence, and instability. The scars she left home with made it difficult to believe in a God who could possibly love her. She did what many of us do and tried to earn God's favor by doing things she thought would please him. The day she discovered the unconditional love of her Heavenly Father was the day she realized she no longer had to work at pleasing Him. She was His daughter and she experienced unconditional love for the first time.

How some of my siblings felt and saw things that took place behind closed doors remains their story if they choose to tell it. How we interpret life is different for each of us. I was sent a very wise saying and it reads like this; "Family is like branches on a tree. We grow in different directions but our root remains the same." Some choose to share their story while others feel it's important to leave it in the past. Without the encouragement of my sisters and other close family members, I may have chosen to leave this book unfinished. I am grateful that some have allowed me to include portions of their thoughts and remarks in this book.

I understand how difficult it must be to undertake a role of a stepparent. Many of you reading this book can identify with the challenges a stepparent is expected to assume in the life of a child who is not their own. I may have found it easier to make some allowances for Ernie's behavior if it was directly related to us not being Ernie's flesh and blood. This was not the case in our situation. Ernie's temperament towards anyone who crossed him was fueled by his desire to be in control at all times, as it was in our house.

Anger, explosive rages, and fear are the inappropriate behavior that best describes what we could expect from him. It became a reality for me in second grade. We were living in Arizona after moving two thousand miles away from where the majority of our family lived. There would be no one who could question Ernie's parenting. The few family members that lived in close proximity were afraid to say anything to him. You would have had to know this man in order to understand the power he wielded over others through fear and intimidation.

I wish I could understand and explain the two sides of fear that defined much of what we lived with. Both proved to have dire consequences not only for us children, but for our mother as well. Ernie would use fear to intimidate us into submission while mother's fear paralyzed her to the point that she would often refuse to stand up to him.

Mother was no stranger to fear. She grew up with a mother who was so harsh and unforgiving at times that fear controlled a large part of Mom's life. Fear is debilitating and often remains a part of a person's personality. We children learned that fear was so deeply-rooted in our mom that she was unable to protect us from our stepfather. As one of my sister's said to me, *"Or mom chose not to."* Though it helps us to understand why she allowed abuse to go on in our house, it didn't justify it. She was our mother and had a responsibility to protect us.

Just exactly where mom was the day I brought my report card home at the end of the school year, is a question I can no longer ask and expect an answer to. I was eight years old and had just completed the second grade. I walked home from school with no idea what was written on the blue paper I held in my hand. If I had any idea what my teacher had written and what awaited me at home I would have thought about running away. That worn out blue paper is still tucked away in my files today and it reads exactly like this, "Janene is still immature and it will be to her advantage to repeat the second grade." My failure to be promoted to the third grade earned me a spanking by my stepfather. My sister still remembers in detail how I was being yelled at and humiliated while I was cowering down in front of him. What kind of a father does that to a small child because she wasn't mature enough to be promoted?

We then moved from Arizona to California where Ernie was able to secure a job working for a sugar beet company as a skilled worker. Some of the most difficult years of my childhood occurred while we were living in this small sugar beet community. It included a little church, post office, store and several streets lined with houses. We spent the next three years living in this community where we experienced explosive outbursts and immoral behavior at the hands of our stepfather. We were left with wounds that could only be healed when we were ready to forgive our abuser.

As a child there was no way to anticipate when Ernie's anger would surface. We were all too familiar with what to expect when he was in one of his moods. He was a master of terror and made certain we were terrified of him. It only stands to reason that if we were fearful of Ernie that our mother would be as well. Though there were many opportunities for him to manifest his anger and fulfill the need to control his house it most often manifested during our supper hour. Being able to express our opinions and engage in family conversations was not a part of our experience around the table. The only thing we shared together during our meal was his hostility.

Our mother often became the target of his outrage. It usually happened during dinner while we were still sitting at the table. Ernie would stand at the sink and if she said anything that upset him he would raise his hand as though he was going to hit her. I don't believe he ever became physically abusive to her as was his practice with his first wife. His threats were compelling enough to make his point. The moment he raised his hand acting out what he wanted to do to her, it would trigger an indescribable anger in me.

Hate for this man began to intensify in my heart. Each time it happened, and it happened many nights, I wanted to jump up, go to the kitchen drawer, grab a knife and kill him. I hated every part of him. I wanted to protect my mother and my older siblings. What I imagined I could possibly do wasn't the issue. My heart screamed, "Don't you touch them!"

My older sister shared with me that my way of protecting them was to be the first in line when we were about to be punished. He often insisted that my sister and I be taken to the garage for punishment. I always sensed it was to avoid the possibility of someone seeing us being mistreated. I never once felt any love behind his discipline!

I was determined to somehow protect my brother and sister from Ernie's outrages. My sister describes me as having a defying personality. Why not! Our birth father certainly wasn't in any position to intercede, even if he had wanted to. The only weapon I could battle Ernie with was my mouth. I of course lost those battles every time. I never stopped to consider he was bigger and more powerful than me. I had already learned how he operated when he became angry and I knew well the cost of crossing him.

I remember being sent to my bedroom to be punished where Ernie then proceeded to force my brother and sister to spank me while he stood by watching as though it brought him pleasure. It somehow never registered during those times that I could never win. Though I knew what the prize for losing was, it never stopped me from trying.

I could spend a great deal of time explaining the trouble I often found myself in. What started out as a happy day easily turned into, "I am in trouble again!" I once accidently hit a neighborhood boy with something I threw. When the Bible says, be sure your sin will find you out, I had no doubt mine would be. Ernie's vocabulary did not include the word accident. I always knew what awaited me whether it was an accident or not. Immoral thoughts running through my stepfather's head afforded him the pleasure he sought when punishing us.

I don't know what led me to be such a rebellious child. It was usually my mouth that caused me the most problems. My verbal reaction to him was quick and sharp leaving no time to take back the river of words pouring out of my mouth. Though I would be the first one as a Christian to tell a young person today the need to respect their parents regardless of whether they deserved it or not, at the time I was driven by the horrific things he did to me. Most of those events I have described took place between the ages of ten to twelve years old; however, little did I know the abuse was not over. What had been done during those three years would have an emotional impact not only on me, but on my sister also for years to come.

I would do anything to avoid going back to the house if it were possible. When I walked out the door to go to school it became a reprieve from the tension I felt at home. Unlike many children today, getting up to attend school was not a problem for me. I was able to walk out the door, catch a bus, and leave whatever conflict may have happened the night before behind. I spent as much time as possible alone by myself. Though our community was small and somewhat rural, it provided the surroundings I needed to escape from the conflict that was often the way of life in our house.

A railroad ran alongside our community where freight cars picked up sugar beets produced by local farmers. The tracks became my best friend offering me the solitude I needed. There was nothing more wonderful for me than to walk those tracks and see where they would take me. Anywhere was better than what awaited me at the house. I was driven with a need to find places where I could be alone. One of my favorite spots was an open field behind our house. I most often walked with my head down in order to discover some missed treasure. I remember thinking that my discovery of a cow skull was like some rare find. Ok, I was a kid at the time! I was alone and safe and that's all that mattered to me. The skull was an added bonus.

—5—
Left Alone Unprotected

IT HURTS TO THINK OUR HOUSE never felt like a home. What was there to look forward to? There were too many plates flying, things being broken, and the ever present verbal and physical assaults. The atmosphere in our house changed as we grew older so it required us to see things with a different heart and different set of eyes. Often the overpowering presence of destructive events taking place made it hard to see the good.

Growing up I never gave much thought to why our mother didn't protect us or why she allowed us to experience the unacceptable at times. She either wasn't able to stand up to Ernie or chose not to. She was there to give us advice and it was never given with any sympathy. Even as grown adults mom would tell us whenever we started to share our woes, *"You made your bed, now sleep in it."* She lived by those words. Did she ever once stop to think we didn't make the bed she chose to sleep in, she did! Did she realize that her children were the ones who paid the price for the bed she slept in? Her choice had dire consequences for us. Every parent should realize that their choice of a partner will have a direct effect on their children. Choose wisely!

It was always spoken and reinforced by mom that what happens in our house had better stay in our house. Any negative emotions that may have been brought on by the abuse we suffered or the things we observed taking place in our house, were to be internalized and silently dealt with. Everything had to be kept a secret! Including a secret that happened one summer which she refused to believe.

Mother made plans to visit her family one summer in Michigan. She would be taking my brother and my baby sister with her and leave my sister and I alone with Ernie. I was ten at the time and my sister was twelve. Looking back, I will always wonder why mom left us by ourselves with a man she knew we hated. Nevertheless, that is exactly what she did. Our summer experience could best be described as, "left alone unprotected." There was no one to question what this man had in mind to do to us. It isn't something I wish to describe neither do I find it necessary. What I will say is this, he did the unthinkable to us. He fulfilled his ultimate betrayal as a man and stepfather in order to satisfy his unrestrained sexual appetite. Harsh words to write? Yes, and difficult!

What made the situation so much more devastating for us was mother's denial that it ever took place. When my sister confided to our aunt what Ernie had done, our aunt went to my mother to let her know. She refused to believe it ever took place. My sister then approached our grandma hoping that someone would listen to her. Our grandma refused to believe it happened and became angry with my sister. I know this occurs in families where children are molested and made to feel guilty by a parent who refuses to believe them. We were left on our own to deal with the effects of such a despicable act. No parent wants to believe these kind of situations happen to their children by the person they are married to or by a family member. It's easier to deny it took place rather than take the responsibility that they somehow failed their child.

Instead my sister and I were left to question if we could have stopped what he was doing. I know for certain that we were so scared of Ernie that he held us in bondage to his desires. In the end we had no choice but to deal with the emotions of what was done to us in silence because the one person we turned to for comfort denied it happened. There was no place to turn and no one willing to listen except our aunt.

I know many reading this situation can identify with what seems to be widespread among families today. It's hard to talk to someone who hasn't been affected by sexual abuse or who has known someone who has. I found myself rejecting certain forms of affection because it brought images I would rather forget. Needless to say I had many issues I needed to work through when I married my husband.

It's rather sad to think we were never given the opportunity as children to experience the hugs and affections that every child deserves to receive from their parents. I left my home environment never fully understanding the hole inside of me that needed to be filled. With the limited understanding I had about feeling loved, I found myself looking for it in places that were not healthy. If my home life presented an atmosphere of love, I may have been able to leave out the chapter on, "He Loves Me He Loves Me Not." I lacked the understanding of what I was supposed to look for in relationships. I left home not loving myself. I never felt a sense of love from the one person I thought I should have received it from. My father certainly did not love me and my stepfather had no clue what love was.

Many times our lives reflect the environment in which we were raised in. If the reflection in a mirror could talk, mine would say, "Janene, nothing you ever did or said was right." There would be many voices in the future that would be in agreement with the way I felt about myself. Voices I allowed myself to believe. When you grow up in a house where there is virtually no remembrance of encouragement or positive input, you learn to walk away with a low self-esteem. The way we feel about ourselves has a profound effect on the way we live and the choices we make. We can't go on blaming our parents for the unhealthy mistakes we make. Somewhere we have to stop the blame game. My childhood wasn't what it should have been and the amount of negative situations I faced made it near impossible, at least for me, to pull the positive times from my memory.

I believe my mother did the best she knew how. She never asked for her husband to walk out leaving her with three children to care for. In the end I'm not sure if in her desperation for help, she failed to really know the man who would be responsible for her and her children. Nevertheless, mom remained married to Ernie for forty-four years and during that time they were able to share many happy memories together. The pressure of raising children was behind them and they had more time to enjoy one another.

Until the day mom died she held so much inside of her that we felt we had a right to know. Mom's refusal to communicate with us left us with a great deal of unanswered questions. I will never understand why mom kept so much a secret and expected us to find the answers and healing on our own. My stepfather was by far not a perfect man, but neither did our mom step in and provide us with a home that felt safe. In the end, we were able to receive the necessary healing to put the past behind us as we learned to forgive.

Should she have allowed us to endure what we did? No! It never took away my love for her or her love for me. There came a time when she was strong enough to express that love without the pressures she often faced while we lived at home.

I am understanding the power we have as humans to bring hurt to our loved ones unintentionally. Writing did not prepare me for having to face my own failure as a mom. Does it surprise us that as we point out the flaws of others with one finger, there are three fingers turned and pointed right back at us?

I needed to learn to forgive both my birth father and stepfather. My stepfather was driven by the demons inside him that had to be satisfied, while my birth father was driven by his sexual desires for women. I would need to forgive both of them and I knew I could not do that in my own strength. If I had not already forgiven these men years before the writing of this book, I would never have openly written what you have been allowed to read. Though I have experienced emotional moments thinking about my birth father not being in my life, I have never dwelt on the past abuse I endured with my stepfather until I was asked to write this book.

Let me explain. When you read the chapter on "Redemptive Lives" you will understand how I was able to forgive a man whom I once hated with every fiber of my being. I first had to understand the depth of my own depravity and my need to be forgiven. The only one who could forgive me was my Savior. My heart began to change over a period of time and though it was gradual, I eventually found it easier to look at others with grace. I was able to lead my stepfather to the Lord and watch a remarkable change take place in his life. He had an amazing change in his heart when he sought God's forgiveness during the last years of his life.

Only those who have been forgiven can possibly understand how a person is able to turn hate into love. I reached a point in my life where I was able to comfortably call Ernie the man I once hated, dad. It would take years before either of us reached the point where we could love one another. All his abuse and anger buried any evidence of love I ever felt from Ernie. It wasn't until I was seventeen that I saw a spark of caring surface from under the harshness that was such a huge part of who he was.

It took place one night while watching the Beatles on television. I found myself struggling to get breath into my body when I collapsed on the floor. I felt Ernie lift me up and place me in the car. I was in the back seat fearful of dying and recalled seeing the speedometer reading near one hundred miles an hour as they rushed me to the hospital. Could this mean, hateful person really care about me? When kids were going crazy over the Beatles I was fighting for my life.

6

Myasthenia Gravis
Was This the Last Night of My Life?

THE DREAMS AND VISIONS I HAD for my life at the age of seventeen appeared nothing like what my future looked like. When I should have been returning for my final year of high school, I instead spent it in a hospital fighting for my life. Though there are many situations we are given the opportunity to prepare for, nothing could have prepared me for what I faced. It is certain that the unknown can often be a blessing in one's life. Neither myself, nor my family would knowingly choose to have the entire picture painted ahead of time of what my life looked like as I struggled to survive.

My ten year battle with this disease started when I was a month away from completing my junior year of high school. When I was called upon to read in class I suddenly found myself unable to finish the sentence I was asked to read. Not only did I not have a voice, I could not move my lips to form the words. I sat at my desk more confused than embarrassed. How could I be a normal student one day and the next I was in a classroom with my classmates staring at me with a look that said, "Finish reading!"

I'm not certain at what point my mother felt concerned enough to schedule an appointment for me to see the doctor. There was definitely something not right about what I was experiencing and we both hoped to have answers to what might be causing these strange symptoms. During our visit with the doctor it was suggested stress was causing my speech problem. Since there was no other explanation given to us at the time it seemed like a reasonable answer. I had been through a great deal emotionally over the last preceding years feeling a little self-conscious about being older and taller than most of those in my class. The situation surrounding my home life was another possibility for what I was experiencing. Mom and I walked out of the doctor's office that day hopeful things would somehow improve. It was only a matter of time before our hope diminished.

Summer break was about to start and I allowed the excitement of having the time off from school to push my speech problem to the back of my mind. My sister was getting married and asked me to be in her wedding. We would both be traveling from California where we were living, to Massachusetts where the wedding would take place. The plan was for our mother to arrive ten days later giving us time to make necessary preparations before the actual wedding. I was still struggling with my speech but hadn't noticed any other unusual changes taking place in my body until after we arrived in Massachusetts.

It was only a few days into our trip when I began to have problems swallowing my food. I started to choke whenever I tried to eat. My ability to swallow became more difficult each day until I was terrified at the possibility of choking and not being able to breathe. It was during one of the eating episodes that I knew something was seriously wrong with me. It scared me enough to know that I needed help. Out of concern for what had just happened, my sister and future brother-in-law rushed me that evening to the nearest emergency room. The doctors and nurses were not certain what the problem was and thought perhaps it might have something to do with drugs. I was still under age which meant my sister couldn't authorize any treatment and Mom was still in California and hadn't yet arrived.

For the next several days I continued to have problems eating and began to lose weight. My body still required food and though I was hungry, every attempt to eat became a challenge. My stomach cried out, but I was reluctant each time to respond. My sister's future mother-in-law was an amazing Italian cook who would always place such wonderful dishes on the table that could tempt anyone to eat. Each mealtime became a struggle between my desire for food and the fear of choking.

It wasn't as though I went about each day anticipating something new could go wrong. I was a seventeen year old going about life without much thought to what might happen next. There was still time left before the wedding to visit some of the historical sites in the area. I didn't want to fly back to California and not get to take in some of the famous landmarks.

With a camera in hand we set out to visit Plymouth Rock where the pilgrims had first landed. My sister handed me her camera and asked if I would take a picture of her and her future husband as they stood in front of the Mayflower. As I prepared to take the picture I realized I was unable to focus my eyes while looking into the camera. My sister became frustrated with me and said, *"For goodness sake, just take the picture."*

I told her, *"Jan, I can't close my one eye."*

She could not understand what the big deal was and neither was I able to explain something I didn't have any answer for. None of us had any clue what I was dealing with or the side effects of what would soon be given a name. I had just learned by experience that I had no muscle control to shut one eye and my other eye was drooping.

It came time to meet the plane that brought my mother to the wedding. I remember the shocked look on her face when she stepped off the plane that day. I had lost about ten pounds since the last time she had seen me. Having never weighed more than a hundred and thirty-six pounds on my five-foot-eleven body made it apparent that something was definitely wrong with me.

We somehow managed to enjoy the wedding before we were due to fly back home to California. I can almost be certain that mom spent the hours on the plane not thinking about how well the wedding went but how she needed to find help for her daughter. She wanted some answers as much as I needed to understand what was going on in my body. I'm not certain how many phone calls she made after we arrived home before locating a neurologist in Santa Barbara, California which was eighty miles from where we lived.

When we entered the office of Doctor Hal Gregg we still had no explanation as to why my body was getting weaker. While I sat on the examining table the doctor looked at me and seemed to know without any explanation from us what I was dealing with. What he did next proved he was correct in what he believed was wrong with me. He asked his nurse to go purchase a candy bar and bring it back to his office. I'm thinking to myself at the time, "if that was going to be for me then I had every reason to get excited." If only I could actually eat a candy bar!

He then proceeded to inject me with a drug while waiting for his nurse to return. When the nurse stepped back into the office she handed the candy bar to the doctor and he in turn reached out and handed it to me. To my absolute delight I was able to eat the entire candy bar without any difficulty. It took one injection and a candy bar to confirm what Doctor Gregg suspected all along. Before we left his office I was diagnosed with a disease called Myasthenia Gravis. I know mom and I were both relieved to finally have an answer. I left his office that day and went straight to the county hospital to be admitted.

During the first two weeks in the hospital they regulated my drugs to determine what would effectively help the disease. The medication appeared to be working and I was able to eat like everyone else. I was doing so well that I was allowed to leave the hospital for a few hours a day as long as I didn't leave the area.

Mom would drive me to the Santa Barbara beaches were we spent time walking along the shore line. I remember we came to a very tiny outlet and my first reaction was to jump over it and that's exactly what I did. My legs were so weak they gave out and I soon found myself lying face down in the sand. It was apparent my body's muscle structure was weaker in places I had yet to experience.

I began a regiment of oral drugs. The medication seemed to be working so the doctor felt it was safe for me to travel home on the weekends but insisted I needed to be back on Sunday night. It was during my second weekend home that I developed a chest cold. I will always remember the television being on that evening and being excited to be watching the Beatles. Truth be told, I believe I was dancing to the music in the living room. At some point that night I began to struggle as I tried to get my breath and I soon collapsed on the floor.

My stepfather placed me in the backseat of the car as he and my mother rushed me to the emergency room. Once I arrived at the hospital mom was able to inform the nurses and doctors that I had just been diagnosed with Myasthenia Gravis. I remember laying in the emergency room as they inserted a tracheostomy tube in my neck giving me the ability to have airspace to breathe. They eventually moved me to the ICU where I laid awake throughout most of the night. I looked to the left of my bed and saw my parents, older sister and brother-in-law standing in my room. I overheard my mother tell my sister and her husband that I was not expected to make it through the night.

I did survive and in the morning my neurologist was updated on my condition. Doctor Gregg called and made arrangements to send a qualified team in an ambulance to transport me to the Santa Barbara Cottage Hospital. If I was scared the night I collapsed in the living room, it was nothing compared to the moment the special team arrived and took me from the intensive care unit to the waiting ambulance. I was moved without any source of air attached to my trach. Though it was not a long period of time, it was enough time to cause me to panic.

While I laid in the ambulance on the way to Santa Barbara I remember feeling this sense of calm as I looked out the window. I had air to my lungs and felt safe for the moment. When the ambulance arrived at the hospital I was all too aware of what this could mean for me if I was yet again removed without oxygen. There was no way I could prepare myself if that were to happen.

I remember being fully awake as they began to remove me from the ambulance. They removed the air supply from my trach and fear immediately gripped me as though this was the end. I thought to myself, this can't be happening. Those very thoughts would be repeated many times throughout the disease. By the time I arrived inside the hospital everything seemed to go black due to a lack of oxygen. I was still alive and could hear voices but nothing appeared clear to my vision. I wasn't immediately given oxygen and had no way of communicating how desperate I was in need of it. Though this would seem really strange in today's medical field not to recognize my need for air, so little was known about this disease at the time.

My neurologist had not yet arrived at the hospital and those who were attending to me were inexperienced on how to help. What the nurse started to do next went very wrong. I heard her say to me, *"This liquid medication will help loosen the cold infection in your chest."* As soon as I felt her hand place a cup near my mouth I realized, this is not good! I had learned enough in two short weeks that this liquid was going straight into my lungs. I was in trouble and fading out fast.

In desperation I reached out into the darkness and felt a hand grasp a hold of mine. That hand was the hand of a heart doctor who immediately inserted the oxygen into my trachea and in essence saved my life. I know today his hand was an extension of God's hand to keep me alive. It's very difficult for me to retell much of this chapter as I feel as though I am reliving this all over again. ♥

I was placed in Intensive Care and remained there for the next seven months living on tubes and machines to keep me alive. Myasthenia Gravis is a rare disease that affects your muscles and respiratory system. When any of us with this condition become sick our natural antibodies are released in us to fight any infection. When that takes place the antibodies in people with Myasthenia Gravis interfere with the nerve signals disallowing them from completely firing. This in turn causes the muscles to not function properly. Muscle control is lost and in most cases like mine you can't swallow, talk or breathe without help and lose the ability to have strength in your arms, neck and legs. You become dependent on medication and machines to do for you what other healthy individuals are able to do for themselves.

I was unable to eat or drink and needed an intravenous drip to supply my nourishment. I had gone from my high school weight of one hundred-thirty-six pounds down to ninety-nine pounds. For ten months I laid in a hospital bed feeling like the only thing touching the sheets were my bones. My inability to swallow made it necessary for all my medication to be administered in shot form. That involved close to eighty shots a week or more to keep me alive.

It would be nearly a year before I was I able to swallow even a single drop of water. I felt deprived of the one basic need that most of us crave besides food. I knew that to cave in to the desire to drink meant the path of that water would go straight into my lungs. There was only one occasion during my entire hospital stay that I begged my mother to help me taste broth by pouring it into my mouth. We both knew it would need to be immediately removed from my lungs, however, she loved me enough to give me that one chance to taste something. Mom stood by ready with the suction machine to clear it from my lungs. I don't regret trying it and was thankful no nurses walked through the door during that time. If only the taste could have stayed in my mouth longer.

It was seven months before I would walk again and ten years before I ever spoke completely normal. Unable to speak and verbally communicate meant that during the time I spent in the hospital I had to find another way to express myself. Not having a voice meant I was defenseless when it came to explaining what I was feeling or the help I needed. If I could take and maneuver one arm to lift the other arm, I was able to have a pencil placed in my hand. This enabled me to slowly write what I needed to say. It wasn't often my muscles were strong enough for me to move my arms to even hold a pencil.

I often wonder as a mom myself, what my mother must have endured emotionally as she watched me lay in the hospital bed day after day attached to machines to sustain my life. She was never guaranteed when she walked through the hospital corridors to the Intensive Care Unit what she would find. There were no cell phones for her to hear ringing with any updates. After working all night and sleeping for a few hours she would make the eighty mile trip over the San Marcos Pass to be with me. She would stay by my bedside until it was necessary for her to return home and back to work. I can only imagine the agony she faced with this illness.

7

The Unrelenting Fight for My Life

MANY TIMES MY STEPFATHER WOULD ARRIVE at the hospital with Mom to visit me. I was still struggling with our relationship. Not much had changed for us though I saw a few indications he might actually have some love for me. It was a picture and feeling I didn't often experience while I was growing up. I remember on this particular visit Ernie kneeling down on the floor next to my bed while promising me that if I lived I could eat whatever I wanted. That remark had nothing to do with not having enough food in our house growing up. I had earned the childhood title "the garbage can."

I was lying in bed fighting for my life unable to eat and his love was manifested once again by those precious few words. I am thankful for the remembrance of those times when I was allowed to see a glimpse of my stepfather's heart buried beneath his tough exterior. I have a better understanding now that each one of us have layers that need to be stripped away in order to see the person God made each of us to be. Ernie was no exception.

One of the procedures that possibly could help improve this disease was the removal of my thymus gland. So little was known about Myasthenia Gravis at the time, and there was no guarantee that this surgery would help me. Mother sat beside my bed one day explaining what this involved and asked me if I was willing to allow the doctors to perform this procedure. Though I know of no other occasion where I was given a voice during the time I was sick, it seemed I was allowed to make this one decision. Her explanation went something like this; *"the doctors will need to open up your sternum which would leave a scar in the shape of a cross down your chest."* In retrospect, I realize she was expressing her concern for how the appearance would affect me as a young woman in the future if I did live. My hope for any improvement made it easier for me to agree to the surgery.

There was a gentleman named Skid who lived in Paso Robles, California who also had Myasthenia Gravis. When he saw all the articles and fund raisers in the newspaper about my condition, he contacted my mother about visiting me. He was a Christian who had experienced his healing and wanted to encourage our family. Several times during my hospitalization he would drive a hundred-twenty miles each way to visit and share the Lord with us. I'm not sure I heard much of what he spoke each time he came. I was fighting every day just to live and yet there was still hope in me that someday I would experience falling in love, marrying and having children. Perhaps my mother's mention of the cross shaped scar had some connection to what she believed I had received spiritual from Skid.

I went into surgery with a team standing by for any possible complications that the doctors might encounter. The surgery went well and I awoke back in my room thankful my eyes were able to focus on my mom still with me. The doctors neglected to inform me that it would be necessary to place me on a bed scale each day to determine if I was showing any improvement in my weight. My chest bone had just been split in two and pulled apart and I thought more than a few times that I would rather have died than have them pick me up to place me on the scale!

Day after day I continued to lay in the intensive care unit hopeful to see some positive changes. Next to my bed stood an enormous breathing machine called an M1. Most oxygen equipment today is built into the walls. I was gradually allowed to be disconnected from the ventilator for very short periods of time. This machine had the ability to save my life and remained beside my hospital bed within arm's reach. If my arms actually worked this would have given me a sense of security. In fact, my arms were useless! I never had sufficient muscle strength to completely lift them on my own and reach the M1.

This presented a problem for me when I found myself alone in my room one day. I found it difficult to breathe and before long my body began to shut down. Without the ability to alert the nurses by pushing the button for help my situation became desperate. The longer I remained struggling for oxygen the more I felt I could no longer even control my body functions. My mother had not yet arrived at the hospital and the nurses had other patients in the intensive care unit to look after. I laid there feeling an absolute sense of helplessness and felt a foreboding feeling that I might not make it. My life support was within reach and there was nothing I could do to save my own life except stare at that machine.

Having given up any hope help would arrive in time, I laid there waiting for the end. Unless my next injection of medication was due, there would be no nurse walking through my door in time. In the moments before I completely yielded to whatever the outcome would be, I turned my head and saw my inhalation therapist walking straight towards my room. He wasn't due to check on me that day. This could only be the hand of God once again making certain His plan for my life was not going to end here. ♥

When the therapist walked into my room no words needed to be spoken. Though I couldn't verbally communicate with him I know he saw desperation in my eyes before he reached my bed. He looked at me and knew immediately that I was in distress. There was no hesitation in what he did next as he attached the breathing machine into my trachea. I believe had my therapist not walked in that day I would not have lived to tell this story. Though there were many days that I would panic for air, this situation was one of the nearest to death I had ever experienced. ♥ It was the only time my body was completely shutting down.

I gradually showed enough improvement that my doctor decided to try moving me out of intensive care to another floor. I would still require a full time nurse in my room and yet it offered my parents hope their daughter was getting better. After so many months in the intensive care unit the slightest change was a milestone to them in my recovery. I had just been moved to another floor in the hospital and knew as long as my mother was in the room with me I would be all ok. I was aware she would eventually need to leave and return home and when she did, my sense of security would leave with her. She lived this disease with me and was more knowledgeable than most nurses as to what my needs were.

My first night out of the intensive care unit turned out to be one of the most vivid days recorded in my memory during the entire time I spent in the hospital. I was still unable to talk, swallow or communicate at the time and my life was dependent on the nurse who was assigned to me that evening. Late into the night and early morning I began having a tough time breathing. I needed the nurse to notice I was struggling so she would hook my machine to my trach. Instead, I watched her pick up a cup of water and knew exactly what she was going to do with it. My body is screaming inside, "No, don't do that." My silent scream went unheeded and once again the water went straight to my lungs. The machine to remove the water from my lungs sat next to the bed, but it was nothing more than a useless piece of equipment if she would not use it. If the medical field knew so little about this disease how was she supposed to know what to do or what not do in my situation? I recall the words my doctor spoke to me towards my release from the hospital at the end of ten months. He said, *"Janene, your life will depend on the knowledge you have of this disease, not the doctors."*

I managed to get through the rest of the night until early morning. I knew I had to find a way to get the attention of a nurse. I needed help and I needed it fast. The nurses were getting ready to change shifts so there was no one in my room. From my bed I could see several nurses at their station but knew I could not wait for someone to come help me. With very little ability to move my body or use my legs, I managed to roll out of bed. I was desperate and could see no other way to get help. While I was trying to reach the nurse's station one of the nurses looked up and saw me on the floor and was able to get help for me. There was no way in the natural that I could have rolled out of bed that morning to seek help. I am constantly reminded as I write my story just how many times my life was being spared. ♥

One night on the fourth floor would send me back to the intensive care unit. What a disappointment this was for my parents. I can only imagine what it took for them to keep hope alive during all those months. I know mom was grateful for every day I was alive and yet I know it had to put an enormous burden physically and emotionally on her. The many months of traveling one-hundred-sixty miles each day only to return to her night job and family could not have been easy for her.

After seven months of being in intensive care I was moved to the county hospital. I had turned eighteen and the state took over the responsibility for my medical cost. My hometown had arranged many fundraisers to help alleviate the financial burden my parent's accumulated due to my medical bills. Although I still needed all my medical equipment, the doctor felt this was the best place for me to continue to get well.

I was gaining more independence from the machine to breathe even though I still needed it at times. When I was able to leave my room it allowed me to regain strength in other parts of my body that had been useless before. I was starting to walk short distances but often found it necessary at times to rush back to my air supply. I was gradually getting stronger and it felt good to be more alive than I had been in previous months.

I was still unable to swallow food or drink water and it was necessary for me to be fed through a tube in my nose in order to get the nourishment I needed. I would wait with expectation for the nurse to walk in my room three times a day with my food. I can picture her now holding a huge syringe filled with a milk formula that would be enough to keep me alive. It made no difference to me at the time as I could not taste anything. Perhaps that is why I have to this day an aversion to the sight of milk.

There was a little bit of defiance in me and I decided one night to try taking a natural breath on my own. I could breathe through the trach with no problem but I had not been able to take a breath through my mouth or nose. I was firmly convinced that I could get away with adjusting my trach valves long enough to experience my first breath without breathing through the trach itself. The trach at that time had cuff valves that hung on the outside of the Tracheotomy. If I took a small syringe and inserted it into the cuff and released the air from the balloons it would allow my airway to open up giving me the ability to take a breath on my own. I quickly took a few quick breaths and it felt so wonderful but I knew I had better hurry and blow the balloon back up before a nurse walked into my room and caught me. It was another wonderful moment in time I wish I could have made last longer.

During the ten months I remained in the hospital I managed to celebrate both Christmas and my eighteenth birthday. The nurses were amazing and set everything up to make room for my entire family. Food was brought in and I stood in line holding an empty plate. No sense making my family feel bad that I couldn't eat.

Although I was unable to enjoy the traditional Christmas dinner I was able to put some weight on with the milk formula they fed me each day.

In addition to all the wonderful things the nurses had already done for me there was one very special day I will not forget. You would think that at my age I was smart enough to tell the difference between real snow and white flakes appearing like snow falling down outside my window. I watched snow drifting past the window of my room only to find out later the nurses went upstairs and poured tide out the window above me. We have all heard the saying, it's the thought that counts. I thought it spoke volumes of the care the nurses showed me during the months I was there!

I was still required to live with the trach and feeding tube even after I returned home. I was not able to attend school for my senior year and felt despondent as I watched my classmates on stage graduating. I lost nearly a year of my life and I was starting to feel well enough to venture out and experience life again. Nothing held me back including shopping with my mom with all the tubes still attached to my body. It was necessary for my feeding tube to remain a part of me until I could swallow well enough to sufficiently eat what my body required. I wanted to live regardless of how I might appear to others. This would prove to be true when I prematurely allowed my hunger for life to lead me down a path I was not prepared for.

I would have to wait until the Trachea from my neck was taken out if I was to completely resume the life I had before I developed this disease. When my doctor scheduled a time to remove my only source of life for the last year, I was terrified! I had always felt a sense of security each night at home knowing I could attach the machine to my trach if I needed to. Both the breathing machine and the machine that kept my lungs clear sat beside my bed. I would no longer have them as a safety net should I need them.

While lying on the operating table fully awake I started to panic. My fear only lasted a moment when I realized I was still breathing on my own when they closed the incision.

I wish I could finish this chapter and say I was completely healed and could move on with life. There is much more to this story that influenced so much of my life and the decisions I made. The truth is, I moved on with life well before I was physically ready. The consequences of this disease would affect my appearance, my speech, my relationships and much of the way I chose to lead my life over the next six years. I was on a path that lead to illicit relationships, alcohol and self-destruction until a love that cannot be explained unless you experienced it stepped in and brought me to my knees.

8

Addicted to Alcohol

I WAS YOUNG AND LIKE MOST GIRLS I looked forward to being married and having someone in my life I felt really loved me. My girlfriend suggested I date a friend of hers and I soon found myself falling in love. I spent my days dreaming about prince charming and our upcoming wedding. Living a fairytale life of a princess is every little girl's dream, but fairytales turn to dust when faced with the realities of life.

In the excitement of joining our lives together Steve and I ignored the health issues we were bringing into our marriage. We spent more time on planning the wedding rather than discussing hurdles we might need to overcome. I was seventeen when a near fatal disease nearly took my life. I spent ten months in the hospital and suffered the effects of this disease for many years. I soon learned that everyday challenges would prove to be more than I was able to handle. My mother who lived this disease with me throughout my illness had tried to discourage us from getting married. Had I listened to her concerns, I could have avoided entering a marriage that had a strong possibility of failing. I was convinced our love for each other was all we needed.

When I first met my husband he shared with me he had been in an accident while he was serving in the military. He foolishly stuck his hand out too far into the street after a night of drinking. The accident resulted in him sustaining an injury that required the surgeons to insert a plate in his head. He would be spending the rest of his life with limitations brought on by seizures.

Steve had been dealing with his condition for a few years before I met him and seemed to handle his disability without many problems. I refused to believe that either of our physical problems were enough to stop our plans to be together. We soon found out dealing with health issues in a marriage was far more complicated than when we were each single.

After we were married things changed rather quickly. Our perfect castle began to crumble. Steve wanted to work to take care of us, but was unable to obtain a driver's license because of his seizures. Jobs with his disabilities were difficult to find. When Steve took a job as a gas station attendant the atmosphere in our home seemed to improve. Most men can understand how important having a job can be to one's self-esteem.

Disappointment was soon to set in for us. While driving home after visiting my mom, I saw an emergency vehicle with its lights blaring in front of me. I somehow knew that those lights were heading for the gas station where Steve worked. When I arrived behind the ambulance I saw that Steve had suffered another seizure. It was hard enough for him to go through the symptoms that accompanied these events, but not near as tough as being despondent over the loss of another job.

If that had been the only issue we needed to deal with in our marriage it would have been easy to work through. Our greatest challenge was yet to come and it was due to the side effects of one of his medications that was necessary to control his seizures. The outcome of this particular drug impacted his ability to be intimate at times. There was no possible way for me to know what this would mean as I had saved myself for marriage. Naturally this led to him feeling like a failure both as a husband and as a man. It eventually became a major block in our relationship and before long our problems began to surface and manifest into arguments that neither of us would win.

We were losing the battle to keep our marriage working. Our house was no longer a home. The way Steve dealt with his mounting frustrations was to walk out the front door. I never knew when or if he would return. Over the next year he continued to close the door behind him many times as I continued to wait for his return. I loved Steve and each time he walked out I wondered if he would remember the directions back to our castle. I vividly remembered the eighth time I watched Prince Charming walk out the door and knew any love I once felt for him was gone. I understood that our marriage was not going to work and I needed to let go.

After months of the never-ending conflicts, we made the decision to separate and eventually we divorced. We both wanted the hurting to stop. I was not the easiest person to live with and my personality lent to many of the conflicts that went on for the year we were married. He was expected as a husband to take care of me when I had issues only the doctors had answers for.

The pain of my failed marriage left me with such an emptiness and loneliness that I felt I needed to somehow find a way to alleviate what I was feeling inside. There appeared to be only two choices I thought would make these emotions I was experiencing any better and I eventually made them both. I would soon find myself replacing the emptiness inside of me with alcohol and men.

It wasn't hard to convince myself that the void in my life needed to be filled. I began my search again for someone who would love me. I had no desire to be alone, and I sincerely felt all that had transpired in my childhood dictated the direction I was to embark on. I've wondered if it is unreasonable to believe that what a person feels about themselves can also lead to the decisions one makes in life.

I began to make my choices based on who I perceived myself to be. I had no self-esteem or self-worth as a child. If love was given it was because there were conditions that had to be met. Looking back I don't believe I met any of them. I wasn't going to change that perception with what I had in my heart to do next. I never stopped to think about anything other than this urgent need I thought I had to fulfill. The demand for love led me to make choice number one and I didn't waste any time looking.

My search began in the bars and nightclubs which lasted more than three years. If I had known what the outcome was before I started down this uncharted journey, I would have chosen a different direction. I was about to make the second decision I felt I had no control over and it wasn't a result of my childhood. I was trying to deal with what this disease made my body look like.

I was walking into every bar with the same physical problems. I would be sitting at a table with a girlfriend and when a guy decided he wanted to be friendly he would approach us and start a conversation. As much as I wanted to fill the void in my life, my greatest challenge with my speech disability just presented itself. Like any future encounters with the opposite sex, they were going to find out I could not talk normal and that I was different from other girls.

As I explained in the chapter about this disease it wasn't that I had to learn to talk again I simply didn't have the control over the muscles in my face. Not only was I dealing with my speech, but my facial muscles were not working either. I talked with my hand covering my mouth in order to hide what I looked like. I quickly figured out if I could drink enough, the muscles in my face and speech were slightly improved. It did not stop me from covering my mouth or hiding the anxiety I was experiencing. I was fully aware of all my issues and no amount of wishing them away was going to change that. Inside of me a battle raged between wanting to run from the rejection I was bound to experience in any relationship or continue to live life regardless of the hurdles I would face.

I convinced myself that reaching for a drink was the only way I could face my emotional state and before I knew it I was no longer in control of my life. I found the more I drank the less anxious I felt and I was able to feel a little more confident. I was a young girl who had been sick and yet still had the same desires I had before my illness. I was faced with finding a way to live with my passion while at the same time admitting to my disabilities and trying to adjust my life accordingly.

Alcohol had taken over and the need to drink became so powerful that I was making choices I would never have made if I was sober. I was now living alone and trying to hold back enough money out of my SSI disability check to supply my need for liquor. My desperation led me to live each night on a can of tomato soup loaded with crackers. Most evenings became a routine for me. I would sit alone at the table eating my soup while thinking about buying my next bottle of whiskey. I can't say I was entirely alone most of those evenings as I had the pleasure of listening to my western music while drinking. The powerful words reminded me of what I wanted and did not have. What a combination for destruction!

My life at this point was one big spiral downhill and I had no clue how much deeper my choices would take me. I am not saying there wasn't anyone trying to discourage me from continuing on the path I was on which was going to destroy me if I didn't stop. The voice of my Mother spoke those same words later when I found myself being locked up for drinking. For now though, I was being controlled by my addiction. When I was not at home I could be found in the local bars while on my quest for fulfillment.

Throughout the next several years I followed the same path week after week going from one relationship to another always taking my addiction with me. I could not function without my dependency on drinking. Looking back, it only made my problems more serious. I was now depressed more than ever as I realized that my excessive drinking and unsuccessful attempts to keep a relationship in my life were leading me to the possibility of committing suicide.

That possibility presented itself one night when I was feeling alone and having to deal with another rejection that involved someone whom I had fallen in love with. Unlike many of my other encounters with men, this was the only other person I had honestly loved. When I met Wally I was not aware that he was separated from his wife and seeking a divorce. When that information was revealed to me it was too late. I fell in love not realizing that there was a possibility that Wally would eventually try to reconcile his differences with his wife.

I thought I had finally found in Wally the missing piece of my life I had been looking for. During our relationship I had taken a short trip back East to attend my niece's baby dedication. Upon my return to California I found out that Wally had gone back to his wife. I heard this news from none other than Wally himself. What I was not prepared for was how to live without this person and how I was going to cope with the feelings I had for him. I soon realized that Wally was willing to give me the time I needed to figure it out. I later learned the hard way how he was going to do this.

Many nights as I sat alone at home Wally would show up on my doorstep knowing that I would let him in and give him what he came for. He knew how much I loved him and that I was not strong enough to keep my door locked. I was offering him the best of both worlds and he was more than willing to take it. Our relationship continued like this until the night he could no longer deal with the guilt he was feeling about what he was doing to his wife. I was not ready to hear the words he spoke to me that evening before he left the house for the last time. Our time together was up and we were no longer going to be seeing each other. I am not sure he had any idea what those words would lead me to do only a few nights later.

One night as I sat at the table with the companionship of a full fifth of whiskey, seventy-five sleeping pills and a bottle of valium I contemplated ending this pain I could not escape from. I was being encouraged by the music I was listening to that had the power to add to my despair. How fitting to be listening to Dolly Parton sing, "I Will Always Love You." I am not sure I really wanted to die as much as I wanted this feeling to go away. I wasn't in the frame of mind to consider that the pain I was feeling would not always be there. I made the decision I was better off ending my life and I reached out to what was in front of me. It did not take long for me to finish the bottle of whiskey while emptying both bottles of pills at the same time. Something was missing in my life and I felt like nothing would ever be right. I was hoping somehow my suicide would let Wally know just how much I loved him. How foolish of me to think I would ever find out the answer once I was no longer here!

While still conscious I made a phone call to my sister who lived three thousand miles away to tell her I loved her. I believed her to be too far away to allow anyone to intervene in my decision to end my life. I remember nothing beyond those few words of our conversation. The pills and whiskey began to distort my ability to reason. I do remember looking out my slider window and seeing my mother and brother pulling up in front of my trailer. I opened the door and stepped onto the porch and didn't have to wonder why they were there. I have no idea how they managed to get me into the car and rush me to the emergency room as I have very little memory of that night. It was only after I awoke in the morning that I realized I was in the hospital and what I had done the evening before.

I spent the next four days in the hospital before being allowed to leave. During that time my mother had contacted Wally to let him know what had happened. I'm not sure if she made that call on the suggestion of my assigned counselor who knew I needed to deal with what had just taken place with my attempt at suicide.

I did receive a visit from him and remembered looking up that day to see him standing at the door of my hospital room. What I felt in my heart at seeing him left me with the knowledge that I would always love him. I don't recall the conversation we had, but nothing changed in our relationship and it would be a few years before we saw each other again. There is no doubt in my mind that Wally still loved me. We were two people who realized what we once had was lost forever.

9

Out of Control

I continued to live a self-destructive lifestyle. Both my desires for alcohol and my determination to have someone in my life continued to propel me in directions that were so unhealthy. My behavior was impulsive and led me to actions that I am not proud of. Anyone looking at my life during this period of time would have felt nothing but distain for me! It was hard for my mom to watch me live this lifestyle and not be able to do anything to stop it. She constantly worried that the day might come when my drinking and driving would cause my death or the death of someone else.

My dependency for alcohol became so uncontrollable I would make sure I had whiskey, coke and ice in the car wherever I traveled. I was an expert at reaching down on the floor of the passenger seat and fixing a drink while still driving. I was slowly killing myself and could not stop long enough to recognize where I would end up. There was only One who had the power to do so and I was not prepared for how that was going to happen.

My excessive drinking influenced my personality and I soon realized that I was choosing men who had the same addiction as I had. I thought I had once again found the man I could love forever. We met in a small local bar in Los Alamos, California where we were both living. We were together for several months before we realized the combination of us both drinking was just not working. I knew we cared deeply for each other, but living together proved to be a huge mistake. My disposition was hard to deal with and drinking drove me to want to continue to argue over every disagreement we had. If push came to shove, I would try to gain the last word and I usually succeeded because Bob wasn't one to argue. I lost in the end when Bob informed me he was leaving to seek a job elsewhere.

I drove Bob to the bus station in Santa Barbara so he could catch his bus to the Santa Anita Racetrack where he would be training race horses. I stood there watching the bus leave with someone I loved and there was nothing I could say or do that would change the situation. Once more I felt the effects of abandonment and was distraught that my life was falling apart. I was such a mess that I found myself desperate to talk to someone! The only person I knew in Santa Barbara was my neurologist and I headed straight for his office.

Looking back, I now realize that the thought to run to my neurologist was placed there by God. It became another piece of the puzzle that God was using to transform my life. The one who had the power to change me was at work and the process was about to begin without me realizing it. This disease that I had was not getting any better by the lifestyle I was living. When my doctor saw the condition I was in he immediately made an appointment for me to see a psychologist.

I agreed to see the doctor and soon found myself in the Santa Barbara Cottage Hospital where I spent the next two months in an open ward with others who also had a variety of issues they were dealing with. During that time I attended the required meetings and saw my doctor each day. I knew I could walk out of that hospital door at any time and go back to the life I was leading. Instead I chose to stay and attend every meeting and counseling session. If anyone during those two months would have suggested that I would finish my therapy only to leave and head for the nightclubs, I would have disagreed.

While in the hospital, I shared a room with a girl who also struggled with drinking. It seemed our common interest in the nightclub scene was compelling enough that neither one of us could fight the desire for men and alcohol. We were both released at the same time and found ourselves heading straight for the bars. We were stopped that evening by the highway patrol while driving back to her apartment. We had managed to pick up some guys at the club and one of them happened to be a lawyer who was sitting in the back seat. We somehow managed to avoid a citation and I realize now that God was again at work orchestrating His next move in my life.

We continued our partying back at the apartment and by morning I was in rather bad shape. I had a regular scheduled appointment with my psychologist earlier that morning and when I walked into his office he knew at once I had been drinking. He looked at me and said, *"You need to go back to the hospital."* My reaction was to run and that's exactly what I did. I ran down the main street of Santa Barbara where I planned to catch a bus back to our apartment. What happened next was the strong arm of the Lord dealing with my unwillingness to make the necessary changes on my own.

While still on the opposite side of the street where I would be catching my bus, I looked at the bench where people would be waiting for the bus going back towards town. There was no one waiting there but on the bench was a wallet. I had always considered myself an honest person so I picked up the wallet and went to a pay phone to call the police. I told them I had found a wallet and where I would be waiting for my bus across the street so that I could give the wallet to them. While I sat waiting I saw a policeman on a motorcycle pull up to the curb in front of me followed by a police car. I turned around to see another policeman coming out of the bank behind me. Unaware of what was about to take place I proceeded to reach out to hand them the wallet only to be handcuffed and placed in the police car.

I had no idea what was happening to me. I was trying to be honest and return the wallet to the police so it could be returned to its owner. One minute I'm sitting on a bus bench and the next I'm sitting in a police car. I was driven to a building that was surrounded by brick walls. I was taken out of the police car and escorted into an unfamiliar locked facility. The police proceeded to remove the handcuffs off me and lock the door barring my way of escape. I had no thought of trying to flee and it wouldn't have done any good if I had tried.

I was now in a place where other difficult people were being held and given psychological help. Instead of the peaceful calm open ward at the Santa Barbara Hospital, I was now with a group of people who I considered mostly crazy. While walking to the room that would be my home for a while, I looked into one of the other rooms and observed someone in a straight jacket. I watched others attempt to jump the wall that surrounded the building while we were allowed outdoor activity. I convinced myself that I had a drinking problem, but I was not crazy and wondered to myself, "What do I do now?"

It did not take long for me to understand why I was brought to this place. After my scheduled appointment that morning with my psychologist he called the police and had me picked up and put on a seventy-two hour hold. Seventy-two hours was all the doctor could legally hold me for, but he left on his vacation and I had no way to be released without him. I wish I could place a piece of the puzzle image at every place I know God was at work, but I trust you can see the hand of the Lord arranging my life and circumstances.

For the next ten days I found myself wondering how I was going to survive this situation. I was given a chance to make one call and I made the call to my mom. I assumed because she loved me she was the right person to call and that she would help me.

Instead, these are the exact words she said to me, *"Keep it up and you'll never get out!"* She said something to the effect that if I continued on this road I was on I would end up being in worse places than where I was now at and would never be able to leave. END of CONVERSATION! Click!! I had just experienced a different definition of tough love.

Once I became a believer I could see how the Lord used every situation I was dealing with as a part of His redemptive plan for my life. I was forced to remain the ten days behind locked doors and had no way of knowing that this situation would change my life completely. While being incarcerated, I wondered how I would remain protected from those I thought were crazy. I spent a lot of time in my room away from some of the most unimaginable people who were in there.

Upon my arrival I was introduced to one of the doctors who took an interest in me and my roommate. When he had the extra time he would check in on us and visit for a while. Through the many conversations we had during those ten days it was clear he really cared about us. When I was released this same doctor and I set up a time to meet for dinner. He was someone I could talk to and I appreciated the wisdom that he would share with me.

We have all heard that God operates in mysterious ways and many times we simply do not understand what He is doing or why. It is only after we see the end result that we are able to realize where He was working in our lives to bring about His purposes. Please understand that what I am going to share with you is not a picture of the way most of us would think God typically works to bring redemption to someone's life. This doctor became one of the puzzle pieces God used to end my addiction to alcohol and who He would use to set me free from all that previously held me back.

I found myself sitting at the Santa Maria California Airport with this doctor who I knew was married. As I think back to that night I don't know what his intentions were or what mine were at the time, but there is no doubt in my mind that it was God's perfect arrangement for us. We enjoyed our dinner and conversation which seemed the normal thing couples do. I no longer felt the need to drink and I knew my heart was changing and that this doctor was a positive person in my life.

For three years I struggled with feeling like I could never be forgiven for my past and yet this man looked at me from across the table and said these powerful life changing words, *"Janene, do you know God can forgive you."* In the years that I lived the lifestyle of a drunk and going from one man to another, I never heard those words spoken to me from anyone.

Why did God use a man who was married and one dinner date to help change my life? I absolutely believe God arranged this date and knew exactly what this doctor would say to me. That night was the last time I saw him. After giving myself to so many men over a period of three years, he was the only person who never asked me for what every other man had asked for. My life was truly changing.

What best describes my life from that night on is pictured below. I was once on a track leading nowhere and in one moment my Heavenly Father used this doctor to help me switch tracks. I was never going to be the same again because my God was not willing to let me go.

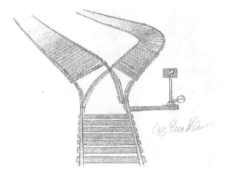

Much of what I shared in this chapter on Addicted to Alcohol is directly connected to my chapter on relationships. I cannot disconnect one without affecting the other. Having said this, you will at times hear me repeat some of the situations previously mentioned as well as those who were involved in my life. I will only mention the names and circumstances of those who played the most significant role in the three years I was fighting this obsession with needing a man in my life and self-medicating with drinking.

When the Lord asked me to share my story with you including the unpleasant circumstances surrounding my life, it was for one reason only, that you come to understand His unlimited grace and forgiveness. No matter what your testimony consist of, there is nothing that can hinder the Father's plan to bring you to Himself.

If you have ever thought about ending your life, I hope you understand there are better options available to you. Anytime you believe the enemies lies about yourself you need to know you are listening to the wrong voice. You have a Heavenly Father that is never willing to give up on you and is waiting for you to trust in His love and His desire to be your Father.

My birth father and my mother

Mom's three stair steps

Jan, Billy, Janene

My grandpa and grandma Fulton

Mr. Skidmore, the man who led me to Christ

Ten months in the hospital

Christmas dinner I wish I could eat

Ten months and finally going home
with my machines and tubes

My dating days

Son Aaron, Daughter-in-law Kelly, Piper, Parker

Daughter-in-law Robin, Coy, Trent, Kali

Daughter Leah & Everett Ashurst
Emilee, Leann, Allison, Cristee, Colton

Daughter Jessica, Jaden, Remi, Austin

My husband Bob

The last time I saw my dad

10

He Loves Me, He Loves Me Not
Searching For Love in All the Wrong Places

"GOOD GIRL, BAD GIRL, My Father's Daughter" are the words that best describe my past life in regards to relationships. I knew so little about relationships in a positive way and like most girls growing up without a father, I was constantly searching for what was missing in my life. Since I had no father who could set the right standard for what I should be looking for, I found myself settling for whoever would have me. Having no understanding of what a healthy relationship consisted of at the time, I blindly stepped out into the dating world.

I was seventeen when I first began to have romantic ideas about falling in love. I had left my first childhood crush back in the sixth grade and was ready to move to something more serious. The emotional needs within me at the time could neither define the word romantic nor understand the meaning of love. My desire to fill the void in my life was so powerful that any distinction between what was real and what was fantasy took a back seat. I learned the definition of both of those words through the painful experiences I went through over the next six years. I was a typical young person looking to be in a relationship with no specific expectation except, please love me!

Exploring my options was a little more challenging since I held no interest in the boys at school. I carried this notion in my head that I was cursed with being so tall and a year older than my classmates and it made me feel uncomfortable most of the time. I had no plans as to where I might start my search to fill the need in my life when I was invited by a friend to visit the USO where we lived in California. The United Service Organization was a club that provided a place for those in the armed forces to gather for a time of fellowship, music and dancing. The ladies who volunteered were there to provide refreshments and to interact with the men who were serving away from home.

Much of my weekends were spent enjoying the friendships I was able to establish with the men and women at the club. It was the first time I felt free to be myself and had no difficulty socializing with those who were older than I was. I was serving as a volunteer; however, I was the one who found a fulfillment I hadn't experienced in the past. I was both needed and valued as a person and I started to see myself in a more positive way.

I soon dated one of the young men from the club that I took an interest in. It was my first real date and I admit I was not too educated in the needs of men. It wasn't long before I realized that not all men's intentions are pure. There was no shortage of opportunities from the time we left town until arriving at the base to find a place to pull off and park. I never allowed myself to get lost in the passion of the moment. Though I dated a few other service men, I managed to keep myself from yielding to temptation. I clearly thought at the time that I was resisting any unfavorable advances in my own strength. It would take looking back to see that there was someone looking out for me that I had yet to meet behind my determination to remain untouched.

There are many pieces to a puzzle ♥ that make up the whole picture of a person's life. As I continue to write portions of my story, I'm amazed to see God's protection and intervention in my life that I wasn't able to see before now. I can picture my Heavenly Father picking up another piece of the puzzle of my life and setting it in place. It became very clear to me through what I experienced one morning while lying in bed at my sister's apartment, who truly was responsible for my resolve to not give into my desire for men.

I remember so well the morning I woke up and watched my sister getting ready for school. She found herself pregnant in her senior year of high school and decided that Tom and she would get married. They moved into an apartment in town where my sister started to attend a different high school while finishing up her last year. For reasons I can't explain I had somehow spent the night with her. I attended an entirely different high school and can only assume I was sick and had been dropped off at her apartment the night before. As I laid in bed watching her getting dressed that morning I remember telling myself, "I will never let myself get pregnant before I get married!" I knew at that very moment I would save myself for the man I would someday marry.

I never understood at the time where those thoughts originated from and assumed they were my own. Regardless of the circumstances that placed me in the bedroom that morning instead of at home attending class is not important. What's important is, where did those thoughts come from if not from me? I may not have believed then as I do today that there is no such thing as coincidences when God is involved, but I now understand that it was those powerful thoughts planted in my thinking and heart that saved my life.

It's certain that we can't possibly know why some things happen as they do. We go through life believing we have all the answers and live as though we have no cares in the world. We spend so much of life as though today is all that matters especially when we are young. I was living my days carefree with little thought about tomorrow until, a few months into my world of dating, the circumstances of my life changed forever. One day I was perfectly healthy and the next day I was diagnosed with a life threatening disease.

What I was not aware of at the time was, if I would have allowed myself to follow my passions with men and found myself pregnant, it would have cost me my life. I know without a doubt as I was looking at my sister pregnant and preparing for school that morning, my intention to not ever get pregnant wasn't something I determined on my own. This was another piece of the puzzle that God continued to place in my life. ♥

Following my release from the hospital I slowly began to enter back into the world I once knew. My enthusiasm to pursue life where I left off before my illness was being complicated by the effects of this disease. Nevertheless, I refused to allow my disabilities to hold me back from putting myself out there in public. I had the same desires and needs that I enjoyed before I found out about the Myasthenia Gravis. For that reason I was determined to endure the stares and somehow find a way to meet my emotional needs.

My girlfriend Linda and I pretty much found ourselves doing what most young girls do and kept our eyes open for anyone that might notice us. We both worked at the coffee shop in town where there was never a shortage of guys stopping in for a cup of coffee. Linda eventually met Stan while working the counter and it wasn't long before they were married. Stan eventually brought his brother Steve in for me to meet and it wasn't long before we fell in love.

Steve and I were married and happy newlyweds for several months. Since most of the details about our marriage were already shared in the previous chapter, I will only talk about a portion of what transpired over the next year. Our health issues coming into our marriage became a recipe for disaster and we eventually filed for divorce.

Divorce was the key word that changed my good girl image and opened the door for me to start down the road that earned me the bad girl reputation. Until my marriage to Steve I had never given myself to another man and had practiced abstinence during the years that I dated.

When Steve and I were no longer married I believed I could no longer be forgiven for my failed marriage. Rooted deeply in my heart was the conviction I had fallen completely out of God's ability to ever forgive me. We have all heard or read the saying, "Eat, drink and be merry, for tomorrow we die." I absolutely believed my ticket to heaven just vanished along with any hope things would change. Nothing seemed to matter anymore! Though I never consciously made a decision to live life like there was no tomorrow that is exactly what I did.

When my father chose to walk away from our family for someone else, it left my mother a divorced single mom raising three children. Though she was not responsible for the situation she found herself in, it became necessary for her to make some tough decisions that would cost her in the end. She could no longer live without some form of birth control to prevent any chance of a pregnancy occurring. Having been raised in the Catholic Church she was aware she would need to talk with the priest about her current circumstances. The church was so adamant about divorce among its people and very much against birth control; however, she decided to plead with the priest to understand her situation and give her absolution. Instead, she was ex-communicated from the only church she had ever known.

I was never able to erase from my mind the price mom paid for her divorce. I felt certain the same judgement applied to me the day I could no longer keep my marriage together.

For years I watched Mom drop us off at church while she sat in the car waiting for us. She wasn't permitted to attend the Catholic Church and was denied communion. The church at that time represented themselves as being the only true religion and therefore man's only security into heaven. For my Mother to believe she was eternally lost was unthinkable to me.

When I became a Christian I was able to identify with the hurt she carried with her for years resulting from what the church called an unpardonable sin in her life. This was exactly where I imagined myself to be when I failed to uphold the only standards for marriage I had ever known. My divorce became the reason for my plunge into a life I am not proud of.

It is not my purpose to demean any one religion for I truly believe if one confesses and acknowledges the one true God and Savior Jesus Christ, then good can be found in the different Christian denominations. I have many wonderful friends in the Catholic Church who very much love Jesus. When the churches hold traditions and rules that are neither ordained nor approved by God, it can have an enormous effect on people. I lived with this prevailing belief what happened to my mother applied to my situation as well. I spent several years living as a divorced women who lost all hope of being forgiven. It was several years before I heard these seven words spoken to me, "Do you know God can forgive you?"

For the next three years I searched to find someone who would fill the empty space in my heart that was once occupied by my husband. I attempted to fulfill a little girl's dream in a grown up world. Soon my fantasy world gradually turn into a harsh reality that I was not prepared for. I was a woman who needed more than my looks to make a relationship work and I didn't have much to offer of what really mattered in one. How could I?

I spent the first seventeen years without an active father in my life. Though I loved my father he chose not to return the love and had neglected his fatherly responsibilities. I wanted to be Daddy's little girl and it never happened for me. Without realizing it I was looking to men to provide me with what my father never gave me.

I had no self-worth and was certainly not a confident woman. All the important attributes that a father can nurture in the lives of their children and especially in their daughters was not available to me. There was no way for me to find that one person to complete my life when I had nothing but brokenness to offer. My moral compass was distorted and it set me up time and time again for rejection. I spent much of my childhood seeking recognition and I continued my search to find it in places that were so unhealthy for me.

I was going from one bar to the next hoping to meet someone who would truly love me. That's all I was ever searching for and those words would be repeated many times throughout this book. Until we find that missing piece we often permit our bodies to be used in ways that demean us rather than build us up. We keep hoping above all hope our search will come to an end when we finally find genuine love. For me, that would take several years of going from one relationship to another. I had begun to wonder if anyone could love me. If I had stopped long enough in my search I would have realized that I was losing a sense of self-worth by the very choices I kept making.

How fitting to title this chapter, "He Loves Me, He Loves Me Not." Did I have an unrealistic view of what love was supposed to look like? My dreams of romance were crushed one right after the other. I am too ashamed to admit to the amount of men I gave myself to in those years.

In order to deal with the constant rejection I was experiencing, my need for alcohol began to drive me deeper and deeper into an addiction I couldn't stop on my own. I was leading a miserable existence and I was so out of control I could not keep anyone in my life for very long.

My body's demand for drinking always found what it needed in the bars I frequented. My preoccupation for finding a man to love me and my desire for alcohol pointed me on one continuous downward path. When a man introduced himself to me I never expected that he was only looking for what my body could give him. I went into every encounter believing that the next man would finally choose to love me. Perhaps my hope should have died, yet instead I never lost it. I guess you could say my hope made me vulnerable to anyone that wanted to take advantage of me. I once shared that those looking at my life would have said, "You may as well have been a prostitute." Perhaps a better description of my life would be, one who gave herself for love at whatever the cost.

At the age of twenty-two I met a man whom I fell hard for. I was so blinded by my need to be wanted that I never took the time to consider his true motives towards me. Looking back I realize our dates were always at his place or mine and always ended in the bedroom. I was being used, yet I felt I couldn't live without him. When our relationship ended it would take years to let go of my feelings for him. Much Like Steve, my relationship with Wally was detailed in the previous chapter.

I decided to make a trip back to Massachusetts to visit my sister. During that time she and her husband had been planning to make a move back to California. It was suggested instead of me flying home I would drive their van. I wasn't going to be traveling alone and my brother-in-law's cousin had decided to travel with me. Terry was somewhat wild in her ways and the combination of the two of us seemed to incite the other into making decisions that put us at risk on this trip.

Our first day on the road Terry decided she knew someone on the army base where we were passing through and decided we should stop in to see him. We somehow managed to remain on the base overnight and were carefully hidden in one of the barracks. The next morning we were back on the road making our way west. At one point on our trip I started to get sick with a cold. This being a serious problem with my condition it forced me to stop at a hospital's emergency room in Texas. I called my mom with my concerns to let her know where I was. She in turned called my brother-in-law who was traveling in his truck to California to let him know what our situation was.

After leaving the hospital Terry and I managed to find ourselves at a truck stop where we allowed ourselves to get talked into putting our van in the back of an empty semi heading to California. I continued to get worse and worried about my physical condition. Our truck driver decided to stop in Moriarty, New Mexico for the night. I was not prepared for what he expected to receive for his offer of help and when I refused he threw me into the cold shower. My first reaction was not shock as much as thinking to myself, this has to be the worst thing that could happen to me with the cold I was dealing with. Needless to say, we would be unloading our van and driving the rest of the trip ourselves.

I arrived back in California and continued to make poor decisions for my life. There was no way for me to escape the cost of my involvement with relationships and drinking over the years. I entered a bar not really knowing much about who I was meeting and who I was allowing myself to get involved with. One such man who I permitted into my life would come with a price tag.

I met Jerry one day at one of our local bars. I knew very little about him other than he loved to dance and so did I. We were truly an odd couple as I was tall and he was short so they called us Mutt and Jeff. We enjoyed our nightclub scene and spent plenty of time drinking and dancing. He had been a boxer before I met him and word had it he had killed someone in the boxing ring. Whether the story was true or not I never gave it another thought until Jerry became jealous and abusive in our relationship.

Jerry had an acquaintance who was a cop in California and had decided one night he wanted to go visit him and his wife. I had a streak in me that never knew when to be quiet and I somehow irritated him while he was driving. I don't recall what I said that night, but he pulled the car over on the side of the highway and proceeded to get out. He quickly came around the car, opened my door, and landed a punch to the side of my head piercing my eardrum.

I had entered into a relationship with a man who could not control his anger. As long as I was compliant to his way of thinking, things were fine. I did not always meet his requirements and it landed me on the bad side of his temper. Jerry did not have to use a lot of physical abuse to instill the kind of fear in me that made me afraid to leave him

One night when he was not at home, I took the liberty to walk down to the local bar in Los Alamos, California where we lived and visited with Dick the owner and bartender. Dick was one of those men who everyone enjoyed talking with. As I sat at the end of the bar having a drink, I turned my head around and saw Jerry walk in the door with a gun. I don't think he intended to do anything with it other than make a point.

The opportunity came for me to devise a plan to have him leave. It was not a foolproof plan but it gave me a reprieve and the time I needed to think about what to do. My uncle drove for United Van

Lines and I asked him if he would invite Jerry to ride along with him on one of his trips. My thought was, "if Uncle Jimmy accidently left him at one of the truck stops clear across the country, he might never return." If you knew my Uncle you would know I did not have to plead with him to do this favor for me. We loved our uncle and he was like a kid at times and so much fun.

My need for a drink kept me walking down to our local bar. I was certainly not intentionally looking for another guy at that time. Jerry was gone and I felt no immediate threat at first. I was always alert to the fact that the day would arrive when he would come looking for me. My anxiety and fear was something I eventually experienced and it remained with me until the day he actually found me.

One evening I found myself once again down at the bar. The corner barstool seemed to have my name on it as it was rarely occupied by anyone else. I managed to earn the nickname Sam and to this day I cannot imagine why. I certainly didn't look like a guy. I remember on one of my many visits that Dick brought this cowboy over to where I was sitting and said, *"Bob, I want you to meet Sam."* It wasn't that I hadn't noticed Bob and his cowboy friends sitting around the table drinking prior to our introduction. Most people generally have an attraction to a certain type of man or woman. I was no different and had always been attracted to cowboys. Bob was a cowboy and I was hooked! But, who was I hooked to?

11

What Was I Hooked To?

Was This My Future Husband?

FINDING LOVE FELT LIKE looking for the pot of gold at the end of the rainbow. Nonexistent! I continued to believe that if I kept looking I would find what every girl dreams about. Love! Was I really living an unachievable dream like the pot of gold at the end of the rainbow or could there yet be someone out there for me?

My attraction to cowboys made it easy for me to say yes when Cowboy Bob asked me on a date the night we were first introduced. We spent the evening talking and discovered we both had something in common besides drinking. There was a time when we had each previously experienced a touch of God in our past. Neither of us had been currently living our lives in a way that would testify to that encounter. Nevertheless, we decided on our first date we would visit the First Baptist Church in Solvang, California.

When I first met Bob he was managing a thoroughbred outfit in Los Alamos, California training race horses. We continued to see each other but omitted any future church dates. It would be a year before either of us stepped into another place of worship. It seemed rather contradictory to attend church when we were living a lifestyle most congregations would frown upon. We were living in sin and were too ashamed to pretend we were fit for church attendance. We never stopped long enough to figure out that church was exactly the place we needed to be.

We would spend many of our evenings at the Maverick Saloon in Santa Ynez dancing and playing pool. I had previously been a bartender in a beer and wine establishment in Santa Maria, California where I had plenty of time to improve my skills at the pool table. We were both in our element as long as drinks were served, music was playing and there was an open table. There was no doubt we were well-suited in the things we enjoyed. Unfortunately, we were both walking the same path of destruction.

I continued to live alone in my own apartment in town and would visit Bob daily at the Petaluma Stud Ranch where he worked. I was living on total disability and unable to work due to the amount of medication I required daily to manage the disease. I was left with a lot of time on my hands which I'm sure contributed to my excessive drinking. There was never a temptation to try any illegal drugs that were available during those years, though I was offered Marijuana. My drug of choice was alcohol. Never once did I stop to consider what the side effects of mixing alcohol with my medication would do to my body.

The time we spent with each other allowed us to see the pain of our past. Bob had been married before and had two little girls who were his life. His neighbors had invited his girls to go to church with them and eventually Bob and his wife Sandy started to attend the church as well. Bob had only been attending the Baptist church for a few months when the pastor asked him to cover a few services for him while he was away. Bob had this natural gift of sharing scripture and at times one would think he had spent years studying.

Bob was six years old when he began having repeated dreams about heaven. He was too young at the time to understand the meaning of the dreams. His family never attended church when he was growing up, so there was no spiritual connection for him to understand what he was seeing. He was only capable of describing what he saw and what he saw were people going to heaven and others being left behind. He never forgot those dreams even though he went on to live a Godless life for many years.

While attending the little Baptist Church with his family in Las Alamos Bob started to sense an awakening in his heart to serve the Lord. Little did he realize at the time this very stirring would cost him his family! Bob accepted the pastor's invitation to preach and was very encouraged by the congregation's response. In his excitement he turned to his wife as they drove home from church and said to her, *"I feel the call to preach."* Sandy turned to him and said, *"Then, that's it for me!"* She stuck her hand up letting him know there was to be no further discussion. Three days later she packed up his girls and drove away for good.

Within a few months Bob no longer felt he was qualified to preach. He lost the family he loved and soon slipped back into his old lifestyle. This was precisely the place where I began to be involved in his life. I suppose I was a diversion to keep his mind off his pain of living in a now empty house. I would attempt to fill the void he was feeling and yet, I knew for months he was still in love with his wife. I felt like the epitome of a one-sided love. I was falling in love with Bob, but his heart still belonged to another.

I would visit Bob at the ranch almost every day so we could spend time together. I remember clearly the day I drove to his home and found him in his bedroom with the door locked. His workers who spoke very little English were trying to persuade him to open it. I knew he was depressed and drinking heavily and it worried me to think about what he might do. I was finally able to get his door open and found him sitting on his bed with a rifle in his hand pointed at his head. I grabbed the rifle and threw it on the floor breaking the stock on it. I had already been at that place in my life where he now was and I knew it solved nothing. He sobered up and never tried to end his life again.

Bob eventually made the decision to quit his job at the Petaluma Stud and returned to Oregon where his parents lived. The now empty house his wife and girls once lived in brought far too many memories that only deepened his pain. I was upset at the thought of him leaving, but there was nothing I felt I could do to stop him. He had already purchased his ticket to take the Greyhound bus home. I chose to remain at my apartment rather than watch him board the bus and leave. I wasn't sure I could handle another failed relationship. Up until this time in my life I had no wins and plenty of losses with men.

Shortly after he drove away I received a call from his friend Johnny Corbett who also worked with Bob. He called and asked me to drive to the bus station and try to stop Bob from leaving. Johnny had learned of an opening at the Westerly Stud Farms in San Ynez were they needed a stable manager. I didn't hesitate to get in the car and drive to town where I was able to reach Bob before he boarded the bus. God apparently had a plan for our lives to be together. It would prove to be some rough traveling before that would happen.

Bob accepted the job as the stable manager and was given a trailer to live in on the property. It seemed more convenient for us to live together rather than me traveling back and forth to where he worked.

My lifestyle choices were difficult for the ones that loved me. I've always said that the choices we make not only affect us but also those who love us. It was one thing for my family to be disappointed with the way my life was turning out and still love me but they had an entirely different feeling towards Bob who they saw as just one more guy in my collection of failed relationships.

I was in need of transportation back and forth to where Bob was working at the Westerly Stud. My parents decided to purchase a car for me. Considering how many cars I had already gone through I thought this to be rather generous. I assume they thought I was responsible because I was their daughter. If my brother was asked how many cars I ruined with all my mechanical skills or lack thereof, he would shake his head and need more than five fingers. My mother often enable me to keep living this lifestyle even though she didn't approve. I realize she did it because she held out hope that I would finally find what I was searching for and settle down.

Our drinking continued to be a daily habit and living under the same roof together brought out the worst in me. Bob went off to work one morning but never returned by evening. He wasn't one to miss work no matter what condition he found himself in. I thought it was strange and I knew there was only one place he could be, the Maverick Saloon! The longer I waited for him to come home the angrier I became. I was obviously without a car because he was driving mine. My temper never stopped boiling and before long I decided to pick up the phone and call the Maverick.

Bob hung out with his best friend Johnny Corbett before I came into the picture and it was no secret I messed up their drinking time together. I made the call to the Maverick and asked to talk with Bob, but of course I was told he wasn't there. I knew differently, but they weren't going to tell me anything to the contrary. I could do nothing but remain angry.

It was close to midnight when I received a call from my parents telling me Bob had been in an accident. The police were somehow able to determine who had purchased the car and had called them. I had no choice but to wait until the next day for my parents to pick me up and take me to the hospital where Bob was. They drove me up to the entrance of the hospital and simply left me to go in on my own. Why they would continue to help me knowing that our relationship was extremely destructive is something I don't have an answer to. Though I was an adult at the time I truly believe my mother held out hope that someday my life would straighten out and therefore she struggled with letting me go.

It was difficult to accept that the man who I thought cared about me was actually stealing my car to drive to Oregon. Bob was so drunk that night he drove into sixteen feet of steel railing and slammed into six feet of concrete barriers on an overpass in San Luis Obispo, California before the car came to a stop. When I walked into his hospital room that morning his entire face and head was covered like a mummy with only his lips and the bottom of his nostrils showing so he could breath.

It was close to midnight when a surgeon who had just returned from Vietnam walked into the emergency room and saw the condition Bob was in. He had laid open his nose completely and had so many head and facial lacerations that required hundreds of stiches inside and outside of his face. The surgeon decided he would work on Bob's injuries. I know Bob counted himself blessed to have someone so skilled doing the surgery. Due to the severity of his facial wounds they neglected to detect a broken kneecap that went unnoticed for years.

My mother eventually returned to pick me up so that we could go inspect the condition of the car. I assume it might have been registered still to my parents. I was stunned to see the entire engine completely sitting in the passenger seat. There's no question in my mind today Bob survived that crash for God's greater plan for our lives to be together. ♥

There were days when both Bob and I knew we could not escape the voice of God causing us to think about the way we were leading our lives. Bob continued to think about his childhood dreams of the rapture and I remember being especially fearful of how wrong it was to be lying next to him and not being married. I had hardened my heart for so long with all my past relationships that the conviction of what I was doing no longer bothered me until now. For some reason God seemed to be doing something in us both yet His voice would often times be silenced due to our continued desire to drink.

The car incident did not turn my parents away from allowing me to find a way to remain with Bob. Christmas had come and gone and it was New Year's Eve. I was staying at my parents that weekend visiting with my brother and his wife who had come for the Christmas Holidays. I hadn't yet heard from Bob and was getting somewhat concerned. The plan was for him to be here to celebrate New Year's Eve with me. When I didn't hear from him I asked my brother and his wife if they would drive out to the ranch and pick him up.

He apparently decided to celebrate New Year's Eve early, real early! All the stable workers felt they could take care of the horses and still drink. At the end of their shift they drove Bob home and carried him inside. When my brother and his wife arrived at the trailer Bob was pretty much wasted. Since he was too heavy for my brother to carry he grabbed his legs and dragged him down the stairs and threw him in the back of his pickup. That is the exactly picture of how he was delivered to me. There would be no need to believe if this story was true if you knew my brother.

Bob managed to sober up and wear the new suit I bought him for Christmas so we could celebrate New Year's Eve together. In spite of everything that happened that day my family continued to tolerate our relationship. Bob had a way about him that even though he was inebriated much of the time he was still fun and likeable. I'm not sure my parent's acceptance of him meant they would approve of us getting married in the future.

I had my own issues that were just as troublesome and inexcusable. Those that loved me saw what I was unable to see for myself. I was fortunate to have my parents close by, though I knew it was emotionally difficult for them to watch their daughter destroy her life. The need to be loved made me reject any wisdom from them.

By all appearances my life was morally corrupt due to my constant drinking and impure relationships. Regardless of the undesirable things going on in my life, there was still positive attributes that remained a part of who I was. I considered myself to be honest and caring and my mother would often tell me, *"Janene, you love too deeply."* The excessive love that I had in my heart towards others was not something I could discard at will. It was a part of who I was and I brought that part of me into every relationship I had.

My need to give love was as powerful as my need to be loved. The love my mother was referring to was a love that blinds you to the nature of what is behind a person and a relationship. It was a little too late at the time to turn back the clock and correct my mistakes. Perhaps my mistakes can serve to enlighten others who are involved in a one-sided love affair!

My relationship with Bob was no different. Even though we had extreme moments of disagreements I still cared enough about him as a person. When he was hurting I hurt. When his character looked bad to others I wanted to help him correct that persona. It's incredibly sad that I couldn't even help improve my own dys-functional image. I made it my job to make his irresponsible acts right again.

I loved Bob and I wanted others to see him the way I saw him when we were not drinking. I started out from the beginning of our relationship making sure he never completely fell in the eyes of others. When I found out he had not talked to his parents for months I encouraged him to pick up the phone and call them. He didn't! I took it upon myself to call and explain who I was and reassure them that their son was alive. Bob was also irresponsible when it came to financial matters. He had more than a few checks overdrawn and I worked at helping him correct his mistakes. Why? Was it just because of my caring nature?

I wasn't trying to paint myself as someone who was without faults beyond my excessive drinking. I had plenty of my own issues to deal with. What I really needed to do was take my eyes off what I thought he ought to correct and turn them on myself. If I had been honest at the time I would have recognized that my caring went beyond love. Since Bob was a part of my life I felt like his mistakes were also going to be a reflection of who I was and I already had plenty of people in my past who saw me in an unfavorable way.

Over the next several months our relationship became extremely toxic at times. Alcohol became the lethal weapon that was destroying our relationship. Bob was never a vindictive person and disliked any kind of conflict. I, on the other hand, never knew when to step back and withdraw from an argument. The dissention between us was escalating to the point that Bob decided to walk away and just leave!

12

Bottomless Pit of Self-destruction

LOSING THE PERSON YOU LOVE can be harder than having them in your life under the worse circumstances. That's exactly how I felt the day Bob decided our relationship was once again over. He boarded a bus for the Santa Anita Race Track where he continued his work with horses. I know nothing would have ever changed in our lives if we had stayed together. Life was dealing me one more blow in the area of relationships and it was my toxicity that pushed Bob away. I felt alone once again and had no one to blame but myself. Nevertheless, it didn't ease the pain of my situation and I hated this void I felt inside.

Life on the Santa Anita Race Track would be the place where Bob would take his final plunge into the bottomless pit of self-destruction. He started working as one of the groomsman and was given the responsibility and oversite to care for some of the most expensive thoroughbred horses in California. His demand for alcohol did not interfere with his job requirements at first until his addiction became so severe that he resorted to eating the horse's feed in order to save his money for liquor.

He had once been both a manager and an outstanding cowboy for some of the topmost known outfits throughout California until his drinking put him at the bottom of his profession. Life for him was declining so rapidly that John Shireffs, another groomsman, said to him one day, *"Bob get your stuff together, I'm sending you home. If I don't, you're going to die."* John bought him a ticket and drove him to the Los Angeles Bus Station. He boarded the bus home to Oregon with one box of his belongings which was all he had to show for all his years of work. John Shireffs is one of the top trainers in the horse racing industry today and we hope to have the opportunity to let him know he was used to save Bob's life. ♥

Bob returned to Oregon and went to work for his dad. Living at home at the age of twenty-seven limited his ability to drink but it didn't seem to stop him. It was apparent in what he decided to do one night that it was going to take something else to wake him up to his addiction. They say once a cowboy, always a cowboy and cowboys enjoy going to rodeo dances. That's exactly what he chose to do that night! He went to the Roseburg, Oregon rodeo dance and got so drunk and decided he was fit to drive home. A motorist noticed him driving erratically on the highway and made a call to the police. He was soon being chased while trying to avoid being caught. He made a turn into a parking lot and managed to run over a log that forced him to stop. The police were so angry they yanked him out of the car and hauled him off to jail for the night.

Bob's father bailed him out of jail and brought him home. In the morning his mom said to his dad, *"Paul, get that boy up and get him dressed. Take him to church! Something has got to change his life."* His dad did exactly that! He got him up out of bed, drove to church, opened the passenger door and told him to get out. Bob walked into church that morning and remembered nothing of what the pastor said, but when the altar call was given he stood up and walked to the front of the church and fell on his knees. He told God, *"If You can do something with this mess, I'm all Yours!"*

Poor self-image makes the climb to the top of the mountain a lot slower. My ascent was hindered by my misconception of what love looked like. I wanted approval for most of my life but received so little of it where it was needed. The need for affirmation dominated much of my life even as a child. I often wondered if at some point in my search for love I felt bad about the way I was living my life, yet I continued to march on relentlessly visiting bed after bed, man after man hopeful I would find what I yearned for.

The transformation of my life from bad girl to my Father's daughter began to emerge the day I was told that God could forgive me. My addiction to alcohol ended when I left the locked down facility in Santa Barbara. I was now forgiven of my past and I knew at that moment what my next move would be. I had to find a way to reconnect with the cowboy I fell in love with that night at our local bar. I never stopped caring for Bob and had not given myself to another man since the day I watched him board a bus to work the Santa Anita Race Track.

We spent so much of our time together in hurtful situations that I lost the sense of love I once felt for Bob. At the same time, I felt a stirring in my heart that I was supposed to marry this man and I wanted to get in touch with him. I had kept his parent's contact information and made that first call to talk with him. Little did I realize when I dialed their number and talked with Bob that he also had reached his lowest point and started to turn his life around. It felt like we were both back at our very first conversation the night we were introduced and had spent time talking about once having known the Lord but had turned our back on Him. Our heart-to-heart conversation proved to be a pivotal point in both of our lives. We discovered through our conversation that both of us had left the old life behind and were starting a new journey.

The challenges I faced were not completely over. Though my addiction to drinking was now in the past, I still enjoyed going to the nightclubs to dance. I will always remember my first reaction when I stepped into a bar sober, looked around and saw how I had once looked. I knew at that moment I would never struggle with that part of my life again.

When I thought all my past struggles were behind me, I encountered a temptation I was not prepared for at the time.

Wally, the man I was willing to end my life for showed up one night while I was out dancing. We hadn't seen each other for over a year and to be perfectly honest with you, some of the old feelings came back to life like a runaway freight train trying to distract me. He invited me to take a ride with him and I foolishly said I would. When it turned into a suggestion that we stop at one of the hotels I knew what was on his agenda.

It took everything in me that evening to say no to him when what I really wanted to say was yes! Those were the hardest words for me to voice, but I already knew where God was leading me. Oregon! I exited the car that evening knowing something changed inside of me and I had every reason to be proud of my decision.

Bob and I continued to correspond and talk about the changes taking place in both our lives. It was during one of our phone conversations that I mentioned to him my mother's concern for my health. She had previously discussed with my neurologist the possibility of having my tubes tied. Mother knew if I got pregnant it would be a dangerous situation. She was never able to stop worrying about me.

I had always longed to have children and this permanent solution wasn't something I would have chosen for myself. When I married Steve it was necessary for me to have an I.U.D. inserted to prevent a pregnancy. There were times I thought if I could remove the device myself I would finally be able to hold a baby in my arms. I would see other mothers with their babies and would think, "why not me!" I was very aware of the danger of getting pregnant with the lifestyle I had been leading. Mother made the appointment for us to see a gynecologist who would be doing the procedure. Both my doctors were in agreement that this was absolutely necessary and we were scheduled to arrive at the hospital the night before this was to take place.

See the following letter dated Monday December 13, 1971.
Portions of the letter are included in this chapter so that you can
fully understand how God protected my life during the years I was
promiscuous.

Hal C. Gregg, M.D.　Medical Neurology
200 East Carrillo Street, Santa Barbara, California　93101
Progress Report
Liby, Janene　　　Monday, December 13th, 1971

*The patient returns voluntarily. She would like to discuss
Dr. Newsanger's recent letter. Her mother, however, came in
first. Her mother wanted to know basically whether Janene
would ever be any better. The thinking was that if she did get
better, then she would be left in a very sterile position, which
would be undesirable. I told the mother I had no way of
knowing really, whether Janene would be any better.
Certainly, I have not seen any change in her in the last three
years. I suppose occasionally one encounters a spontaneous
remission but certainly there has been no evidence of that
here. She still requires large amounts of daily medication to
survive.*

*I told them I thought it was important to have Dr. Walter
share this with me. The issue is whether she should have her
tubes tied. According to Dr. Newsanger's letter, this would be
a relatively simple procedure. It should be noted carefully
that her mother very frankly points out that the girl is
becoming more and more eager to love somebody, have
somebody to love her. She really does not care whether it is
for a day, a week, or a night, and her mother has painfully
faced this.*

I told them I would make the necessary arrangements with Dr. Walter, ask him to contact the patient and kick around with her the idea of having her tubes tied. The principle involved is that she is going to have intercourse somewhere, sooner or later, and my thinking is that pregnancy is a dangerous situation for this degree of Myasthenia Gravis.

Doctor Hal C. Gregg

Prior to our scheduled surgery I decided to Visit Bob in Oregon. I had not seen Bob since he boarded the bus in Santa Barbara, California for a job at the Santa Anita Race Track. It had been over four months since we last laid eyes on each other. If there was a possibility of us ever developing a relationship I wanted to meet his parents who I had only spoken to over the phone. I instantly fell in love with them and they made me feel as though I had known them forever. They were very supportive of our plan to be together.

It was during my visit with Bob that we talked about spending the rest of our lives together. He had joined the Baptist Church after his ill-fated night in jail. It was time for me to travel back to California and get prepared for surgery. I remember Bob calling me prior to surgery and telling me he felt strongly that God wanted us to have children. He spoke to his pastor and ask his church to please pray that the procedure would not take place.

Though I was old enough to make my own decisions concerning the Tubal Ligation that would leave me in a very sterile position, I respected my mom's concerns about my health and well-being if I were to become pregnant. When a mother spends ten months day after day wondering if her daughter will survive, it's only normal for her to be concerned about future complications. My chances of surviving a pregnancy as you read were not favorable. Mom couldn't handle one more heartache. Out of my concern for her we kept my appointment.

Mom and I arrived at the hospital the night before so I could be prepped for surgery the following morning. While we waited for the pre-op nurses that morning my doctor walked through the door and said *"Get dressed your leaving the hospital."* Mom and I were in disbelief! Astounded would be the appropriate description of how we reacted after hearing those words! Could this be happening after going through all the preparations necessary for the surgery the night before?

We had no answers as to why this was happening until it was explained that my neurologist was confused about why I was at the hospital. I had previously broke my shoulder socket when I fell off a horse and was scheduled to have work done at the University of California, Los Angeles. Most of my health issues would require me to have any necessary work done at specialized hospitals where the doctors were more equipped for my rare condition. Though my neurologist approved the Tubal Ligation to be done at the Santa Barbara hospital, he somehow became confused and thought I was having my shoulder worked on at the wrong hospital.

My gynecologist did everything he could to explain to Doctor Gregg I was not having my shoulder operated on, yet he refused to listen to him. My mother was not about to drive eighty miles home when she knew this was nothing more than a misunderstanding on Dr. Gregg's part. She felt certain she could straighten this matter out if she called him. In the ten months that I was in the hospital my mother became very close friends with my neurologist. She drove to a pay phone and called his office and was taken aback when he would not even talk with her. It was apparent that Bob's desire for children and the church's prayers were the reason for the confusion. There can be no other explanation for what took place. It would be another piece of the puzzle showing us that God had a different plan for our lives. ♥

We made arrangements to get married and knew I would have to face breaking the news to my mother. I realized there would be no excitement on her part and I was fooling myself if I believed differently. I'm living that moment even as I am writing the details of that day. She was driving through town as I sat in the passenger seat preparing myself for her reaction to my news. I finally found my voice and opened my mouth and said to her, *"Mom, Bob and I are getting married."* I would describe that moment as seeing my mom's head jerk and hit the roof of the car by my announcement. There was no enthusiasm on her part that day at what I considered to be exciting news for me.

I was asking her to agree to my marriage to a man who only recently began putting his life back together. There wasn't enough time for her to feel encouraged that the changes we were both making would last. I knew it would take time for mom to see we were determined never to return to the destructive lifestyle we had once spent years living.

13

Journey from Rebellion to Surrender

WHEN I CHOSE TO MOVE TO OREGON to further my relationship with Bob I knew my mother wasn't completely supportive of my decision. I felt as though I was starting on a new journey leaving behind the person I no longer wanted to be identified with. The more I continue to share my story the more I realize there is much of my life after I became a Christian that I would rather keep to myself. It seems enough that the good girl, bad girl shared her story to the world. Now that I'm the Father's daughter I would think it only right to keep this between the two of us. I'm learning that His plan supersedes my own desire, so I press on hoping others gain from my mistakes. I continue to learn that surrendering one's life is not always easy or comfortable.

When I understood that I could be forgiven of my past it started a new chapter in my life. I would be misleading you if I said my life over the years was made perfect the moment I yielded and responded to an invitation I knew I didn't deserve. Quite the contrary! I wasn't always a nice person and I still have much work that needs to be done in my life and apparently He wants me to come clean. It's only what we choose to hide that the enemy of our lives will use. When I switched railroad tracks the day I no longer was being controlled by alcohol, I couldn't possibly see where the new set of tracks would be leading me.

When I arrived in Oregon I found an apartment and started working at a truck stop diner and bar. Though there was no longer a temptation for me to drink, I did find myself struggling with the attention I received from many of the truck drivers. I knew in my heart that God was directing my life to marry Bob, yet I was still trying to deal with the lack of sexual attraction that I had once felt for him. I knew it had nothing to do with who he was or how he looked. Each time I decided to sleep with a different man it took away from what marriage was supposed to be between a husband and wife. It would take the Lord's help and forgiveness to restore what I had given away.

When I started to feel as though I was getting weaker in my resolve not to seek out any more relationships, I immediately knew I needed to quit my job. The temptation was starting to win out and I didn't like the way I was feeling. I realize that temptation can be a struggle that many of us may face at one point in our life. I certainly recognized where my human tendencies seemed to be directed and I didn't want to allow them to set me back on a path I would rather avoid.

I fought the impulse to lie to myself that I could handle this job and any enticement that came with it. There seemed to be a battle at first going on inside of me and I wondered at times who would win. I hadn't made a final decision about what to do when I was asked to cover the bar for one of the waitresses. It was clear the first night that I worked that the waitresses and the bartender had agreed to pocket the money for one drink into a kitty for every three drinks the bartender made. If I hesitated before making a decision to quit, I certainly knew I couldn't agree to steal from the very people that employed me.

Sometimes we need the extra help to push us into making the right decision. I made an appointment with the owners and confessed to what was going on and gave them my notice. The conviction about what was wrong and what was right in that situation was easy for me to make.

The choice to not work another job seemed to be the safest decision for me. I was able to keep my apartment on the income I received from my disability check. I missed not having the little extra money I was allowed to earn, but I found ways to keep busy. Bob and I looked forward to spending our evenings together. I wanted Bob to be my husband and I trusted in time we would bridge the gap that I was feeling. I remember the day I received a word spoken in my heart that I was to marry Bob. It would be that very word that would be like glue during our difficult years that kept me from running away from my marriage.

We knew so little about the changes that were happening in our lives at first. We faithfully attended church and became involved where we were needed. It began to feel like we had quickly gone from the frying pan to the fire overnight when it came to understanding this new relationship we had with the Lord. The changes seemed so supernatural that we were soon asked to be youth pastors.

It wasn't as if we went from sinners to saints overnight even though we never intentionally made a choice to sin. We were on a road we had never traveled before and were learning as we continued to walk it. Had we been able to see what struggles we would face in our marriage and family in the years to come, we may have chosen a different path at that time. It's true you can't get from one mountain top to the next without first going through the valley. There were many valleys we would have chosen to avoid if possible, yet those valleys became the places where God was shaping our lives.

We decided to wait six months to get married so our families could attend. My parents were more comfortable with the idea that we were finally changing our lives and were in a much healthier place. It wasn't only my mother who believed in the changes we were making, but also my grandmother, who during the years I was living a self-indulgent lifestyle refused to have anything to do with me. It wasn't that she spoke those words out loud in front of me. She disdained the lifestyle I was leading and being her granddaughter she didn't excuse my behavior. She was my grandma and the lack of love I felt from her was painful to accept! Now that my life was changing she decided to attend our wedding as well.

If we thought life together would be a bed of roses we soon learned that marriage came with its own set of problems and challenges. I was married to a man who showed me what true unconditional love was and on the other hand I only understood conditional love. It's what I grew up experiencing and therefore the perfectionist in me had an entirely different set of standards I placed not only on my own life also but on the lives of others. This contributed to many of our problems and it would take years to undo what was so much a part of who I was.

It can be painful to admit that my past played a tremendous part in shaping my future. I thought leaving a life of sin behind would make a difference in who I was. Not entirely so! I was beginning to understand that much of what shaped my life resulted from not only my childhood, but from my own personality I came into the world with. I'm not certain "unique" would qualify for a description of who I was. Little did I realize that change does not happen overnight just because one makes a commitment to turn their life around! Who I was before and who I was coming into my marriage was not looking much different. My future prospect for a great marriage would depend on my willingness to allow the necessary changes in my life.

When we repeated our marriage vows they included for better or for worse and the worse often won out. I know Bob never complained or saw what I saw in myself. If he did he would only speak to the Lord about it. My lack of validation in life was so powerful that my current nature, disposition and temperament were damaged goods. Positive qualities and virtues would have to come later if I could find a way to love myself and see my worth in the eyes of my creator.

I simply didn't enter my marriage with the knowledge on how to love this man the way a wife should love a husband. I had nothing in my past that I could glean from as an example of what a good marriage should look like. I saw the slightest imperfections at times that seemed to overpower how good this man truly was. Today I understand that those imperfections were nothing more than an illusion to my distorted way of seeing things.

If I was feeling any love as a child it had to be the result of something I did right. I projected those same conditional requirements on my husband that I received as a child. I don't want to harp on my past woes as a child due to my home life as those you are already aware of. I simply needed to understand why I failed in some areas at being a wife in the beginning.

If I took the time to look back I would have to admit that I wasn't a very loving person. I felt incapable of loving myself and easily rejected any positive words directed at me. Countless times over the years Bob has told me how much he loves me. There has not been one day in our marriage that I have not heard those words spoken from him many times. He had an amazing set of eyes that saw beauty in me I could never see in myself. In contrast, I saw every imperfection and no amount of telling me I was beautiful made it easier to receive.

The powerful voices of the past were there to remind me of everything I ever did wrong. It was as though I had stored them in my memory bank and they became the inner voice of self-criticism. It felt like there was a battle within me that was fighting for control to see who would win. Was I worth loving or was I a complete failure? I needed to work at removing the layers that hid the person the Father made me to be. It would not be easy and it wouldn't happen overnight. It took years to shape me into who I was before I came to love the Lord. I knew it would take years for the Lord to do the work that needed done in my life. Today I'm still a work in progress.

Though our past life left much to be desired, we found without the alcohol we had much in common. We enjoyed being together and were both committed to the Lord's work. The qualities that were once hidden beneath our drinking began to manifest in positive ways. I regret that the one aspect of my marriage missing in the beginning was the lack of passionate feelings I should have felt towards my husband. It never kept us from our moments behind closed doors. If you doubt those words you have only to read the chapter on, "My Three Miracles."

We continued to grow in love for one another. We would spend very little time apart in our entire marriage throughout the years. Bob once again accepted the call to preach God's Word. We would spend the rest of our lives moving from one side of the country to the other. California to New England became our training ground, both for the ministry and for our marriage.

I'm thankful I never again had to feel abandoned by a man. I woke up one night not long ago and realized for the first time I had the picture of true unconditional love living in my home. Not once in all of my past relationships had I ever experienced unconditional love. A love that overlooks all the flaws and still stands by you till death do us part. When I think about all the times I used the word love in recounting my past I realize I had no clue what love looked and felt like until Bob came into my life.

I never made it easy on Bob. He lived with a woman who was both harsh and insensitive at times. I was quick to point out what I considered were defects in our marriage and several times I wanted to run from my commitment. I was living with a man who ninety percent of the time would ask for forgiveness when it was really me that needed to speak those words.

His story over the years is his to tell. There is so much I still want to share with my readers about my life and the transformation over the years that brought me to the place where I am today. I hope you won't stop reading this book here.

—14—
My Three Miracles
A Step of Faith against the Unknown

MY GREATEST DESIRE ONE DAY BECAME my greatest joy. Bob and I had been married a few months when I made an appointment with a doctor to remove the intrauterine device that prevented me from getting pregnant. I knew I was risking the possibility something could go terribly wrong if I were to get pregnant. My husband's faith was as strong as the longing in my heart was for a child.

I was able to conceive without any problem and felt I was made for motherhood. My excitement was short lived when I became aware something was not right with my pregnancy. While in a women's meeting at church I received a word from one of the ladies suggesting in a gentle way I might lose this baby. Leaving the church that afternoon I felt as though God was preparing me for what happened.

I went to bed that evening and during the middle of the night I knew something was wrong. I woke up my husband and told him I thought I was miscarrying. I was three months into my pregnancy when I lost my first baby. God prepared my heart for the pain and disappointment I felt. I was determined to not allow this loss to prevent me from having other children.

We were living in a basement apartment and none of the windows would open. I began painting the apartment when we first moved in and the fumes from the paint could have resulted in my miscarriage. I was not one to give up on my dream of having children.

I would lay in bed at night having a conversation with the Lord concerning the baby I lost. It was too early to know whether I was carrying a little girl or a baby boy. I was a fairly new Christian and didn't have all the answers to some of the questions I was asking. Many nights I would lay in bed wondering if my baby was too tiny to be taken to heaven. It was always on my mind until one night I had a dream and my sister was holding my daughter in heaven. It put my heart at rest and made me realize how personal and caring God is even when we are not expecting it. I did wonder why it was my sister holding my baby in heaven as she is still very much alive today; nevertheless it was a moment that helped bring closure to me.

I knew I was testing the waters with my determination to have children despite the consequences this disease could present. Several months after my miscarriage I decided on my own to cut back on my medication. I neither felt led to consult with my doctor nor discuss it with anyone other than my husband. I had been taking forty pills a day for six years to control the side effects of Myasthenia Gravis. I started by cutting the pills in fourths, then I would cut them in halves each time my medication was due. I continued to do this until I realized one day I no longer needed my pills.

It wasn't as though the symptoms of the disease completely disappeared. There were side effects that remained a part of my life for the next ten years. The weakness in my facial muscles kept me from speaking full sentences without difficulty. I was very self-conscious and would cover my mouth to avoid the way my face looked. I also found I needed to help myself swallow food by using my figures against my throat. Nevertheless, I remained off of all medication and decided it was time to release my Social Security Disability Check back to the government. It would be a tremendous step of faith since we were living on very little each month while Bob was enrolled in Bible College.

During the first six months without the governments help I remember walking to the store and searching the grocery aisles for the best deals. Our dinners consisted mostly of hotdogs and an occasional meal made with chicken. The one pleasure we indulged in each night was a small piece of cherry cheese cake. We somehow made it last through most of the week. I knew I would have qualified to continue receiving help for the next ten years. I felt challenged that if I would release my Social Security Disability check it would be a step towards my healing.

Thirteen months after losing our baby girl I discovered I was again pregnant. We were both thrilled and hopeful the pregnancy would go well. On October 19th, 1976, my water broke and I was on the way to the UCLA, Los Angeles hospital to have my son. Though we were living in Glendale, California at the time I was required to do all my appointments in Los Angeles due to the Myasthenia Gravis.

I was not allowed to experience any labor that would jeopardize my ability to breath. It was necessary for the doctors to give me a complete block due to the weakness in my respiratory system. My son Aaron was delivered completely by forceps and weighed in at nine pounds one ounce. What joy we felt over knowing what a miracle birth he was. I only wished my mother could have rejoiced with me each time I called to say I was pregnant. I never heard her once express any excitement over my news. I knew it was always in the back of her mind that I might not survive a pregnancy. She of course was always happy after my babies were born.

The miracle of his birth did not stop there. All throughout my pregnancy my brother-in-law Carmen would say, *"If you give birth to a baby and live through it, I will accept the Lord."* Actually he said, *"If this miracle takes place I'm going to hang onto one of your legs and go up to heaven with you someday."* My sister and brother-in-law had concerns whether I would safely be able to deliver a child. They were both at the hospital the night I was rushed to the emergency room when the doctors told my parents I would not survive the night. Though it had been a few years since that time they still worried about me. When the nurse walked out to inform them I had a healthy son they were ecstatic.

What I didn't anticipate was the attack that would soon follow my release from the hospital. I had always been a perfectionist when it came to my house so I started immediately cleaning in preparation for my parents visit. I was never able to sit in a chair without noticing some imperfection that needed my immediate attention. Two days after giving birth to my son I started cleaning the bathroom floors. I didn't take long before I knew I was in trouble.

My joy quickly turned into total panic and fear. I immediately felt as though I was struggling to breathe and insisted I needed to return to the hospital. When I arrived and was given oxygen my fear subsided. The doctor could find no medical reason he could see that would cause me to have shortness of breath. I would soon learn the power of fear and what it was capable of doing if I allowed it.

Fear would grip me until I thought I was going to literally stop breathing. If there was silence for even a moment my mind would take me to places that would paralyze me. If my husband was not sitting beside me reading the Bible I would panic. The minute he would stop and silence returned I would immediately get scared and concerned for my life.

The feeling of not breathing would come and go at times. Just when I thought the attacks were over the enemy would take me back to the days when I was in the hospital and struggling to breathe. I remember one day several of our Bible college friends were visiting. There were six of us gathered together one night praying and the enemy whispered to me, "There will only be five left because you're going to die." This went on for months until I learned to do battle in the Spirit. It would be a battle I would face again when on May 30th, 1978 I gave birth to my daughter Leah.

The overwhelming desire for another child was enough for me to forget the struggle I went through after my son's birth. I was hoping for a little girl and would spend months dreaming of holding her in my arms. We were now living in Danville, California assisting in a church under Jim Hayford. My pregnancy went two weeks past my due date and while playing badminton my water broke.

I remember that day as though it was yesterday. My sister and brother-in-law were visiting us at the time. When my water broke I knew I needed to place a call to the hospital to let them know. The nurse's response suggested I had plenty of time for a shower before leaving for the hospital. She did not understand I was two weeks late and lived forty miles away. This didn't sit well with my brother-in-law who insisted Bob get me into the car immediately and drive me to the hospital. I would later thank my brother-in-law Carmen for that wisdom.

Bob wasted no time driving me to the hospital while I laid in the back seat thinking to myself, you need to hurry! The trip required us to cross the Bay Bridge into San Francisco with little time to spare. I arrived at the hospital with no time to move me to the labor room. The doctor looked at Bob and said, *"Have you ever delivered a baby before?"* His response was, *"Only the four legged kind."* The doctor and Bob delivered our daughter a half hour after arriving in the emergency room.

My delivery was the talk of the hospital staff the following morning. The doctor that delivered Leah didn't have time to realize I was already on alert for any medical problems that might occur. Instead, he assumed I would be fine walking from the emergency room to the room I would be staying in. Truth! This isn't something that is remotely seen in our current medical facilities. The doctor had no time to check my medical history that would have alerted him to the problems that affect my respiratory system during delivery.

Most reading this will never understand the fear that often dominated my life at times. I felt like the enemy would use every opportunity to remind me what it was like to struggle for every breath. I would maintain a sense of peace as long as my husband was in my room. I knew Bob had to return home to be take care of our son and that thought alone started me panicking.

When he could no longer stay I watched him walk out the door and immediately felt that my security was leaving me to fight this battle alone. When I became anxious and scared the doctors would provide me with oxygen to calm me down. Once I knew Bob was at home I would dial the house and beg him to stay on the phone with me. His voice would immediately dispel any fear I was feeling.

My husband's presence during the difficult times in my life provided me with a source of strength and comfort. I know it was his love and relationship with the Lord that provided me the reassurance I needed. My fear subsided shortly after arriving home from the hospital. The fear diminished as time went on as I learned how to combat the voice of the enemy.

June 1st, 1981 miracle number three was born. We were living in Massachusetts and I was doing well physically and needed no additional oversight during my pregnancy. Both Bob and I shared our different desires as to what we were hoping this baby would be. I wanted another son while Bob was hoping for another daughter. While I was doing the hard work delivering a baby, Bob of course stood waiting to see what the sex of the baby was. My husband looks up at me and says, *"I guess that shows you who is delighting themselves in the Lord!"* That was my announcement that I had just delivered a baby girl. I'm not sure his comment was something you gloat over after seeing your wife going through labor. This was the only pregnancy I never felt an ounce of fear following the birth.

My first responsibility as a Christian parent was to dedicate each of my children back to the Lord. They were powerful reminders of what I would never have had the opportunity to enjoy if my Neurologist had not been confused the morning that I waited to be wheeled into the operating room to have my tubes tied. What should have been a simple procedure that would have kept me from ever having children, was prevented because the man I was to marry believed that God wanted us to have children.

Today my children are grown with children of their own. I often times wonder if they truly understand that God had a purpose for each of them to be born. I look at them and realize that if it weren't for answered prayer to what should have been a permanent situation Aaron, Leah and Jessica would not exist today. Neither would my thirteen grandchildren who are my greatest joy in life.

Being a parent can provide us with challenges we never thought possible. Two of my children one time or another compromised their spiritual walk with the Lord. One struggled with an addiction to alcohol, the other with relationships. Many times in the past I have heard the expression that Jesus died of a broken heart. There were days when I cried so much I thought for sure if I didn't stop crying my heart would literally burst apart.

I have seen and experienced the gifts each of my children have. My son Aaron has served as a worship leader in churches in New Mexico, Texas, California and Arizona. He has been given the gift and anointing to lead people into the very Throne Room of God. He was a part of a worship team that was asked to travel to Africa with Rodney Howard Browne for a revival meeting. Aaron earned his Bachelor's degree in theology and music in Texas.

Having been gifted with the opportunity to serve the Lord with his many gifts has also been an opportunity in the past for the enemy to pull his heart in different directions. When those paths cease to bring honor to the Lord I would stop and remind myself that I had dedicated my children back to God and that they are ultimately His children. It has given me strength and hope for God's redemptive work in their lives when I needed it.

My daughter Leah, has been a blessing as all my children are. She is a gifted worship leader and has a purity about her that resonates whenever she sits down at the piano. She is an amazing wife and mother and a successful business woman. She has a heart that is ready to serve wherever she is needed.

My youngest daughter Jessica has had her share of problems in the past and has used them to turn her life around. My heart felt so broken at times watching the daughter I love making so many unhealthy choices. Today I have the joy of seeing what God is doing in her life. I have every confidence that Jessica will once again use the gifts God has given to her. She is an amazing minister of God's word and I believe that gift will once again be restored.

I am a mom who has every reason to be grateful for my children. None of this would have come about if not for my husband's answered prayer and the misunderstanding at the hospital I believe God was responsible for so long ago.

—15—
Redemptive Lives
Freedom into the Light

THE EVENTS AND INTIMATE DETAILS that took place in my life have been openly shared with you. Allowing my story to unfold in the pages of this book hasn't been easy when so much represented the destructive years I went through. Writing about my experience as a child would involve members of my family. This weighed heavily on my heart knowing that those who choose to read this book may find it difficult at times. Those portrayed in the chapters of this book represent their fathers, mothers, brothers, sisters, aunts, uncles, and grandparents. For that reason this chapter on Redemptive Lives is the most important one throughout this entire book.

The Lord not only brought amazing changes to my life but the lives of those you have read about. If I wasn't able to share the transformation that took place in each of them I could never have continued to write my story with the knowledge it was going to be published. Who I was and who they were in the past isn't the way God wrote the end of each of our stories. My prayer is that the exposure of our lives will help you see how God has forgiven us and allowed us to also forgive the ones who have wronged us. I wish for my readers to see the forgiveness, redemption and the Father's unfailing love by the way He brought change to each of the lives you have read about.

If you were to choose to stop reading here and set the book down you will have missed the most amazing stories yet to be told. Some find it easier to read the pages of a book when it's both thrilling and exciting. My journey represents the negative and the positive side of life. To those of us who have experienced the remarkable transformation that occurred in our lives will find this to be the most exciting part of our story. Our past struggles became our testimony to show the love and forgiveness available to all of us through Christ.

My Life: There is no further need to explain the changes that occurred in me over the years. My life has been an open book for those who choose to read it. It's important to clarify that none of the changes would have taken place if I had not given my life over to the Lord. I was incapable of stopping the destruction taking place as I was determined to destroy myself with alcohol and men. Today I am a child of the Most High God. I am His daughter, He is my Father.

The relationship I share with the Father today did not happen the moment I said yes to the Lord. Healing needed to take place in my life over time in order for me to forgive those who wronged me. Even more so, I also needed to forgive myself and those I hurt in the selfish way I chose to live. Beneath the layers of our lives, I truly believe good can be found in each of us. Removing those layers can only happen when we willingly surrender our lives to our Creator.

If we are to experience the kind of intimacy with the Father He desires to have with us, we must deal with any unforgiveness we harbor towards others. Regardless of what has been done to us in the past or by whom, we must realize and acknowledge that we are all sinners and in need of a Savior. We are all born into sin as a result of Adam's sin in the Garden of Eden. I believe those mentioned in this book have a story of their own to tell. Here is a portion of what I know about their lives.

My Birth Father: When I asked my birth father's daughter if she would share her thoughts with me about my father's relationship with the Lord I received no response. I knew she was a Christian and perhaps could have shared insights with me about the last years of my father's life. Looking back I remember visiting Dad and meeting his friend Roger who was a pastor. Dad was good at construction and helped Roger work on his church building. I believe there was every possibility during the time they spent together that Roger talked to my dad about the Lord.

When I last visited my father I heard his wife share that my father was driving a bus for the Baptist Church their family attended. He enjoyed picking the children up and taking them to church each week. I can almost see him behind the wheel laughing and having fun with the children.

My father had been divorced previously and for some reason the church told him he could no longer drive the bus. I know we are not to be angry, but I see and hear of churches that turn hearts away because of their prejudices towards the sinner. How very sad it was for me to hear this and I hope that did not discourage my father from a possible relationship he may have had with the Lord. I hold out hope that I will have the opportunity to have a reunion with him in heaven someday where perfect love resides and the past is buried.

In truth, my father didn't lead the best life, but neither did many of us. Writing has allowed me to let go of the pain I often experienced when I thought about not having my father in my life. I wish it could have been different but it wasn't. I'm thankful writing has given me a sense of love for the man who was my birth father. If only the clock of our lives could be turned back so we could repair the damages we inflict on the ones we love.

My Stepfather Ernie: The man I once hated became the man I learned to love and call Dad. Having the opportunity to take my readers from the person my stepfather was to who he became in the last years of his life has been my greatest joy. The story behind my years with Ernie was extremely difficult for me to write about. Never once have I looked back over the years and felt anything but love for the person who did the best he could to raise us. Not once as a child or as an adult did I ever hear him talk bad about my birth father.

What he did to me was very wrong but I understand man does what his flesh desires and until a change happens in our lives, we often do things we later come to regret. Following my Dad's conversion I often wondered why he never asked me to forgive him. I can honestly say I never felt I needed him to speak those words, yet knowing how much he came to love his Lord caused that question to surface in my heart occasionally.

I remember Dad wasn't doing well and had been admitted to the hospital. I flew to California to visit him and was very concerned and wondered if he was going to ever be well enough to return home. It was time for me to make a decision about flying back home so I had asked his doctor if dad was going to pull through. The doctor was unable to make that determination at that time. I decided I needed to return to my own family and walked into his room to say goodbye. Dad looked at me with those eyes and a smile that could not be matched by any other and reached out to take my hand and said, *"Will you forgive me?"* I had already taken care of that several years before and simply said, *"Yes I forgive you."* I returned home and never saw my dad again.

My stepfather shares a moment in his writings when he first began to change his life. It happened when I was in the hospital and had come to accept Christ in my life after reading a book that was given to me. In his own words Dad shares the day he was confronted about his relationship with Jesus. Though it took years for him to apply this new found truth in his life, he eventually experienced the transformation as I had.

His own Words written over forty five years ago and penned to paper in a collection of his writing.

Sixteen years ago, my daughter was confined in Cottage Hospital in Santa Barbara in the intensive care unit with a serious illness called Myasthenia Gravis. It was a disease of the paralysis of the nervous system. One evening as she laid upon her hospital bed she called us to her bedside and placed her finger upon the trach in her throat and painstakingly asked this question; "Mom and dad! If I should die could I expect you two to meet me in Heaven?" I was stunned!

I had never given much thought to that phase of my life. With much love and concern she proceeded to share with us the good news, the Gospel of Jesus Christ. How God loves us and so does Jesus and why he came to earth to teach us and save us through repentance and obedience. Needless to say I accepted Jesus Christ as the Lord of my life and Savior of my soul and promised my little girl that I would walk in my Lord's way.

Since that time I am happy to say that my daughter has recovered from that illness that had such a high mortality rate and is now living a happy and productive life in Christ.
—Ernie Kecskes

When Dad turned his life completely over to the Lord he never turned back. It didn't completely happen in the hospital room that day. Like myself, his transformation took several years. When I ended my destructive years and changed my life, my desire was to lead my family members to the Lord. I set out to write each one in my family a letter and encouraged them that they needed to be saved and walk with the Lord. Religion could no longer take the place of the relationship the Lord desired from each of them. In time my entire family accepted Christ into their lives.

It seemed like my dad could not get enough of studying the Bible and learning about His Lord. **I want to conclude this part of his life with another of His writings.**

> *The evening I invited Jesus Christ into my heart. What an entrance He made! It wasn't spectacular, or an over emotional thing, but it was very real for me. Something happened at the very center of my life. He came into the darkness of my heart and turned on the light. He built a fire in the hearth and banished the chill. He started music where there had been stillness, and He filled the emptiness with His love and fellowship. I have never regretted opening the door of my heart to Jesus Christ and never will.*
>
> *In the joy of this new found relationship, I said to Jesus Christ, "Lord, I want this heart of mine to be yours, and I want you to settle down here and be perfectly at home. Everything I have belongs to You. Let me show you around in the body and house of my life."*
> —Ernie Kecskes

My Stepfather's biological daughter: You may recall a letter written by Ernie's biological daughter in the chapter "House not a Home" She shared how her life growing up was filled with unpleasant memories. Her parents would come home drunk and fought constantly. In the midst of an unstable home life she will tell you that she loved her dad. The following are the words she wrote in an e-mail to me concerning the changes her father made in his life when he allowed the Lord to take over.

Good morning dear sister, I remember dad calling me in his later years and asking for forgiveness when he got sick. He asked me why I thought God was keeping him alive. My reply was that God wasn't thru with him yet! I reminded dad that he had a testimony to give and that everyone he met he told them about his Triune God. How awesome is that?
—His daughter Betty.

Words from my little sister about her birth father, my stepfather:

This is how I remember my daddy. I recall a man who was truly a changed person from my little girl days to the man who found God and His Son. He was witty, affectionate, and generous with words of love. I would not know God the way I do if I hadn't had this man as my earthly father! I miss all the wonderful times I had with you Dad. I knew I was the apple of your eye and every time I walked through the door I felt valued and loved.
—Love your daughter Kay.

I can't begin to tell you how many times my sister and I each claimed to be Dad's favorite. When I would visit Dad at the hospital I would write on his chalk board, "I love you Dad" I would sign it, "Janene, your favorite daughter." Later Kay would stop by the hospital and erase what I wrote and make sure she wrote that she was Dad's favorite. We still go back and forth today and laugh about who really was. Neither one of us has a paper to prove it although if you remember what my dad wrote you will have read how him say, "I was his little girl."

My Mother: There is no doubt in my mind writing any damaging remarks about my mom was the most difficult for me. I loved my mom more than words could ever express. Much of what I wrote concerning the years we grew up and the events that took place in our home was not something I thought about as a child while growing up. Having to write my life's story forced me to look at situations I had never understood before and ask questions that I had no answers to.

In my eyes as a child my mother could do no wrong. When I had to describe my childhood and the events that occurred in my life I realized she was not perfect. I had to face the truth that Mother at times chose her husband over protecting us. Surely this was not my mother that I was writing about. How could it be! Why had I never seen it before telling my story?

No my Mother was not perfect, but I know my Mother always loved me. Much of life was difficult for my mother just as it had been for her children living at home. She loved me through my illness and through the years she was forced to watch me destroy my life. Mom found Jesus and never failed to share her love for the Lord to whomever would listen. I remember Mom at the end of her life telling us she didn't want anything said at the funeral except that she loved Jesus. I miss you so much Mom.

I have treasured this very special card and note she wrote to me and I wanted to share it with you.

Dear Janene, Each word in this card is so true. I have enjoyed the years of raising you, watching you grow from the most beautiful baby to a beautiful young lady. We had a few trying years. When you were ill and in the hospital it was hard on both of us. I wanted you to live no matter what the conditions would be and when you finally were able to come home I was the happiest mother in the world.

I don't think you knew how much my heartache I shared with you as you returned to the world you left two years till now. It was the most difficult time of all your young life and yet, it was those trials and downfalls that led you to the full need of God in your life. As we look back we can understand now how He can make someone beautiful where all looked hopeless. He now shows others hope thru you. He prepared you for the ministry you now have in so many ways.

Because of your deep and concerning love for all your family we have all turned our lives over to the Lord. Yes, Janene, my memories of you are always in love and close in our heart. Happy Mother's day.

—Elaine Kecskes

When we stop resisting the Lord and give up our life for His, we will all be able to share our story and give hope to others. God turned our messes into the message I have shared with you.

16

No Longer a Broken Vessel

THE PRODIGAL DAUGHTER: The picture of what awaits those who surrender to the Father's embrace as our life moves from one location towards the veil of intimacy. We find an attachment to the world, a struggle to let go of what vies for our attention in everyday life. We barely live the life God has for us. One day we wake up and find we have wasted the Father's goods. Now there is nothing left and the only one who can restore us is our Heavenly Father. We reach the limit of controlling our own life and discover it's not really living at all. We realize we have walked away from God and that He has left us to our own choices. Our heart condemns us and yet when we are spent, we come to ourselves and realize this is not how our Father intended our lives to be lived.

There is only one thing left to do as we realize we can't go on living like this if we are going to have a relationship with the Father. We awake to the thought that the Father has everything we have need of, and it's time to return to Him. We struggle within ourselves wondering if our Heavenly Father can still love us after defiling ourselves in the worst way. You plan to tell the Father you have sinned by walking away from Him and not making Him your priority in life. You wasted the gifts He has bestowed to you because everyday demands crowded out His purpose for you. You no longer feel worthy of His love. You must make a decision to humble yourself and go home.

Little do you realize the Father has been waiting all this time for you while you were still deciding if you wanted the Father to be the most important person in your life. It's only after His embrace that you realize how much you avoided the one person who would never stop loving you. You ask yourself, "Why and how did I make the choice to walk away in the first place?"

As you approach home you can't believe what you are seeing. Is the Father really running to meet me? How come I never realized before how passionate the Father was towards me. I've made everything else so much more important and yet the Father is hugging and kissing me. Doesn't He see the filth I am covered in? I've just come from living with the swine. How could I be experiencing such affection and love? I tell Him, "Father, I am sorry for sinning against you and heaven." He makes no mention of my sin or what I have done to shame Him. He starts lavishing His goods on me.

I realize that He is the Prodigal Father lavishing me with everything, and I deserve none of it. My heart starts to condemn me, but I remember the scripture that says, "God is greater than our heart and there is no condemnation to those who are in Christ Jesus." He covers me in such a way I no longer remember the way I left and what it took for me to come to myself. He was making me feel so alive in His presence. How could I have ever put anything in life above Him?

I was that prodigal daughter. This is my story.

17

He Who is Forgiven Much Loves the Most

THERE WAS A WOMAN who had greatly sinned who heard that Jesus was having dinner with Simon a religious leader. While Jesus was sitting down to eat, the women brought her alabaster jar of fragrant oil and stood at His feet behind Him weeping. She began to wash His feet with her tears and wipe them with her hair. She continued to kiss His feet and anoint them with her expensive oil. Much to the Pharisee's dismay, he thought to himself, *surely, if this man were a prophet he would know what kind of woman this is who is touching Him, for she is a sinner.* Simon could not conceive that a true prophet would associate with this kind of woman. The kind of woman I was!

Jesus discerning the Pharisee's thoughts answered and said, "Simon, I have something to say to you. There was a certain creditor who had two debtors. One owed five hundred denarii, and the other fifty. And when they had nothing with which to repay, he freely forgave them both. Tell Me Simon, therefore, which of them will love him more?"

Simon answered and said, "I suppose the one whom he forgave more."

Jesus said, "You have rightly judged."

This is the exact picture of my life before and after I was forgiven. He who is forgiven much, loves the most!

I was in my darkest place in life when Jesus chose to forgive my past. I deserved death and instead was given a new life.

Throughout scripture I see the hand of mercy over those who were caught up in a lifestyle that others were quick to condemn. I see myself in the woman who was caught in adultery and brought before Jesus by her accusers to be stoned. Jesus reaches down and writes in the sand, "He who is without sin among you, let him be the first to throw a stone at her." One by one the men departed knowing they were not free of sin. Jesus turns to the woman and says, "Woman, where are those accusers of yours? Has no one condemned you?"

She replied, "No one Lord."

Jesus spoke to her and said, "Neither do I condemn you; go and sin no more."

I entered the ministry with my husband shortly after we were married and we both continued to serve the Lord in various capacities. I realized one day when I was called upon to teach a seminar on the "Father Heart of God" that my struggle to know Him as Father seemed so distant. I would often stop studying and lift my head up towards heaven and ask. "How can you ask me to teach on the Fatherhood of God when I can't be certain that You could possibly love me?"

I desperately wanted to know what it felt like to have His Fatherly love. I would often sit and talk with my little sister and hear her tell me about the conversations she would have with her Heavenly Father. Most of her talks with the Lord took place when she would take her daily walks. When we would sit and have coffee together and share about the Lord the love my sister felt for the Father would just emanate from her spirit. I knew her heart belonged to the Lord and our times of sharing together left me happy for her, but it left an emptiness in my own heart for what I still didn't have. I had been saved longer than her and was responsible for leading her to the Lord, yet she had a depth in her relationship and communion time with the Father that I so desired more than anything.

I never gave much thought at the time as to why my little sister had this wonderful experience of intimacy with the Father that I didn't possess. Looking back I realize she was fortunate to have both a mother and father in the home. She was born after my mother and stepfather married and had both in her life until they passed on. That's not to say she didn't experience difficult times with her father's moments of rage. It was more a result of what she saw rather than being the recipient of his anger. She was his little girl and was blessed to have come through the rough beginnings with her dad and still find a deep love for him as she grew older.

I now understand that my struggle for acceptance from my Heavenly Father was the result of the rejection I felt from my own father. Would I have another opportunity to find a remnant of love hidden beneath the man that was my birth father? My experience in the final moments with him became a painful reminder that there was no love to be felt. I had flown two thousand miles to say goodbye and the rejection I felt was harder than I can possibly explain. What I wasn't aware of during my time in Michigan was what the Heavenly Father was arranging in order for me to finally understand my worth in His eyes.

While in Michigan to say goodbye to my father for the last time I decided to do some shopping with my sister-in-law. It wasn't that we were necessarily poor but we both loved to shop at any thrift store we could find. On this particular day I walked in the store and headed straight for the used book section. Flying on trips didn't leave much room in my suitcase for big items, but I always had room for a book or two. I reached for a book called Created to be God's Friend by Henry Blackaby. It was written about the life of Abraham and how he became God's friend.

I flew home, read the book and by the time I was finished reading it my struggle to see myself as someone the Heavenly

Father could love was over. From that moment on my life began to change in so many ways. I felt as long as my Heavenly Father loved me I could endure whatever came my way.

When I had the opportunity to share this story while speaking at a Woman's Aglow I was asked what the title of the book was. I knew so many men and women struggled as I did with the Father's acceptance of them. They were hoping if they could read the same book it would end their search as well. I knew this was not the case. My response to them was, "never give up believing for what you desire and in time the Holy Spirit will lead you to the answer." I had flown two thousand miles to say goodbye to my birth father and instead found a Father who would never stop loving me. ♥

My involvement in church ministry over the years resembled the life of Martha who spent her time serving while her sister Mary sat at the feet of Jesus. If there was work to be done I made it my responsibility to oversee that everything was perfect and functioning as I thought it should be. In the process, I found myself insisting that things be done my way. It's hard to admit that the perfectionist in me found it difficult to let go of ministry until circumstances provided me with no option.

My husband was dealing with many health issues and it became necessary for him to step down as the senior pastor of our church. It sent me into panic mode as I wondered where that would leave me. For thirty-eight years I had been serving the church and it was all I knew. Ministry at the church had become my life and I was left to contemplate what I would do under these new circumstances I found myself in.

Bob was stepping down and all I wanted to say to him was, "What about me!" It felt like my identity would be left at the church when I walked out the door. It was one of those times in my adult life where the choice was made for me. We were a ministry team and together we left our positions as pastor and co-pastor and sought God's direction for the next years of our life.

Stepping down from church responsibility opened my eyes and heart to a life I never knew was possible. It wasn't until we were no longer responsible for shepherding a church that I was able to see my personality had a lot to do with why I became so involved in the work of the ministry. I somehow felt keeping busy in church guaranteed that I had God's approval in my life. I couldn't possibly see it any differently until I was removed from that position.

My Martha personality was about to be transformed into a Mary. It wasn't too late for me to realize I had spent so many years as a co-pastor keeping myself so busy that I had no time for intimacy with the Father. My activity literally silenced the voice of God. I was so preoccupied with the doing I never stopped long enough to hear His voice speaking to me. I had virtually given no time for intimacy. I sabotaged myself and had no clue that I missed out on some of the greatest moments I could have shared with the Father as His daughter.

I chose to live like the prodigal son's older brother in Luke chapter fifteen who lived his entire life in his father's house and had available to him all his father's possessions for the asking. Instead, the older son never took advantage of the relationship he could have shared with his father. Through my many commitments to the church I neglected the Father who was waiting for me and I couldn't see it. I felt like the Apostle Paul who thought he was doing the right thing in persecuting the Christians until he was struck down on the road to Damascus. Religion often times replaces relationship and like Paul, I was religious without relationship. It took the Lord stepping in and altering my life through circumstances in order for me to have the relationship I now experience with the Father.

Not until I spent quality time in His presence was I able to mourn the years I neglected the most significant person in my life. What the Father longed for was for me to live in His love and instead I kept running to pursue the things I thought He wanted from me. I refuse to return to the lifestyle I once had that kept me so busy I had no time for what really mattered in my relationship with the Lord. Now I desire nothing more than to wake up in the morning and spend time in His presence. Like David, I know my heart and flesh fail Him and yet my prayer is to make the Lord the strength of my heart and my portion forever.

I accepted an assignment to write a book about Intimacy with the Father. I started in 2012 and published, *God's Path to Intimacy* in 2013. I was shown through scripture the pattern for worship that God designed in the Tabernacle of Moses. It involved the steps the priests were to take in approaching God. Hebrews tells us that the Tabernacle of Moses is symbolic for our day.

For years I would blurt out my prayer request for the Lord to answer before I would even give a moment to acknowledge through praise what a wonderful Triune God I serve. The book literally changed my life and I found it difficult to put my name as the author who wrote it. It should have been written that the author was the Holy Spirit.

I found many were reluctant to take the necessary steps to approach intimacy with our Lord. Like so many today, it becomes a challenge to spend the kind of time it would take to walk through the steps while worshipping and honoring the attributes of a Holy Righteous God. I understood that! The steps have become a way of life for me during my devotional time and I often find it hard to leave the Table of Showbread where I am able to thank Him for all He is in my life. I was recently encouraged when I heard Pastor Cho do a teaching on the steps taken in the Tabernacle of Moses.

There were times when I wondered if I truly had heard from the Lord concerning writing God's Path to Intimacy. I hadn't heard much feedback on the book concerning those who may have found a renewed and powerful time of Intimacy with the Father after taking the steps. When I became discouraged I only needed to look at how the book has changed my own life.

18

Memories of the Father's Love

WHEN I WAS EIGHT YEARS OLD I remember walking into the Catholic Church preparing myself to go into the confessional to speak to the priest about my sins. This was one of the seven Sacraments of the church and we followed it without question. I wasn't exactly sure at the time what I needed to confess. I hadn't yet recognize I was considered a difficult child and should have much to repent of. While I stood waiting for my turn in the confessional I clearly recall looking up into this beautiful enormous ceiling and saying to myself, *"Why can't I just talk to God? Why do I have to speak with a priest?"* I had no way of knowing that day where those thoughts came from. The words I silently spoke were soon forgotten and hidden in the recesses of my mind until I became a Christian. It was later that I understood the Father placed those thoughts in my heart as a child in order for me to realize later in life where He was putting eternity in my heart. ♥

As part of the church's rituals I followed the example I was taught and stepped into the confessional to speak with the priest who was hidden behind the barely visible net. I of course remember nothing of what I said that day or what I was required to pray in order to be forgiven. I exited the little room and proceeded to kneel at the altar, slip my money into the box, light my candle and pray to Mary while staring in awe at Jesus hanging on the cross. We were never encouraged to read the Bible for ourselves so I was virtually clueless as to what God expected of me. Like many today, we left it up to the church to instruct us and never would think about questioning it for ourselves. When I became a Christian I was able to see such contradictions to what I was taught as a child.

I neither found lighting candles nor praying to Mary anywhere throughout the entire Bible. Countless times I would walk down the walls on each side of the church praying to the saints only to discover nowhere in the Bible are we instructed to pray to them.

I later became familiar with the Bible and read where scripture clearly conveys to us that the only one who can facilitate our communication with God was our Lord Jesus Christ. To Him alone are we to bring our petitions and confessions. It only made sense that if Christ meant for us to pray to anyone else for our needs or to make confession to someone as a means to communicate with God, He would have indicated this to us in the Scriptures. I am grateful for the opportunity to live out the truth of God's Word as I know it today.

The more traditions placed on man by the churches only make it more difficult for people to respond to Jesus. Jesus's acceptance of me required nothing more than for me to say, "Yes to His invitation and please forgive me." Many who have been immersed in religion find it too simple just to ask for forgiveness without any added religious requirements.

Regardless as to whether I completely agree with the doctrine of the Catholic Church I do want to communicate to my readers that I believe there is much we can learn from the Church. Those who have a personal relationship with the Lord are our Christian brothers in the faith. I know many of them who have a deep love for the Lord and who are the example of how the church touches many lives. There is a reverence in the Catholic Church that can't be found anywhere else. The church has stood as staunch supporters of the right for life and have opened their doors through Catholic charities to meet needs regardless of church affiliation.

What matters above all else is knowing that Christ desires a personal relationship with all of us regardless of what name is above the doors of your church. Jesus found me in the Catholic Church as a little girl and proceeded to lead me to places that prepared me to think about God in my later teens. I will always be thankful for that first recognizable puzzle piece of my life that has the Father's DNA on it. ♥

Our little community was holding a vacation Bible school. Most of the kids saw this as an opportunity to alleviate the boredom we always seemed to experience at times throughout the summer. I was ten and my sister was twelve that summer. The church was organizing a poster drawing contest and were giving away a trip to camp for the first prize winner and a Bible for the second prize winner. Both my sister and I entered the contest. She came in first place and won her trip to camp. I was the second place winner and won this amazing Bible that eventually had my name engraved on it. If you knew my ability to draw or lack thereof you would have to assume my sister and I were the only ones who entered the contest. Perhaps the hand of God drew whatever my poster portrayed as another piece of the puzzle he was placing in my life. ♥

Today I often think about that Bible and wonder if it could be sitting on someone's book shelve or buried beneath the earth. I was very young to be handed this beautiful blue Bible that today would be considered huge for a child my age. The contest took place so many years ago and I still see myself being handed the Bible and the excitement I experienced when I saw my name written on it. I apparently spent time reading the Bible as is evident by my next encounter with church doctrine.

My mother started attending a Lutheran church when I was in my teens. I loved that my mother was now able to sing and attend a place of worship with her family. I remember standing next to her and looking with admiration and joy as she sang out the words to every song. I am not sure how wonderful my mother's voice was, but I always figured by the time our voices reached the ears of God they somehow sounded beautiful.

One Sunday I watched a baby in the church being baptized by the sprinkling of water over his tiny head. I knew that water baptism took place after one confessed their sins. It was not something that I was taught but what I had apparently read in the Bible. I approached the pastor and questioned why he was baptizing babies when the Bible clearly said you had to first ask for forgiveness before being baptized. I knew babies couldn't do that.

Now hold on! Before you start thinking I am out to knock every church I went to. Not so! What I do claim to be is, a person who questions the validity or authenticity of what I believe to be true in the scripture. In this case I was a teenager who knew very little but remembered reading about John the Baptist. You know, the guy who baptized those who confessed their sins. It wasn't like I walked up to the pastor and said, *"Hey, what do you think you're doing baptizing babies who aren't old enough to repent?"*

I would have to believe God was preparing me while I was fairly young to not compromise His Word later on as an adult. I'm often challenged in my refusal to side with those who choose to change what is written in the Bible in order to justify their lifestyle. Perhaps any rejection I felt as a child prepared me to receive it as an adult when confronted with opposition. Rejection certainly doesn't feel good and I can only imagine the rejection Christ felt in His years of ministry on earth.

I was now seventeen well on my way to experiencing the challenges of life only to find myself lying in a hospital bed. Though there is nothing to add to what you have read in previous chapters, I felt it important to remind those reading this book where I knew God was working at keeping me alive for His greater purpose. The next three examples have to do with the months I spent in the hospital. They are the ones that clearly stand out to me.

Having been moved from the ambulance to the emergency room in desperate need of air I began to panic as darkness seemed to engulf me. Hearing but not seeing, helpless and unable to communicate due to the trach, I did the only thing I could do and reached out my hand. At that moment my hand became my silent plea for help. I needed air to breathe and no one seemed to know how to help me. I felt a hand grab ahold of mine and I instantly felt this surge of hope. There was no clarity of my vision for me to notice whose hand I tightly held onto. I refused to let go until I felt air going into my lungs. That hand belonged to a heart doctor who immediately hooked the oxygen to my trach. Without a doubt the hand of God was keeping me alive once again! ♥

It's difficult for me to describe the feeling I experienced the day I laid in the Intensive Care Unit and felt my body begin to shut down. I had apparently been off my breathing machine for a short period of time. I found myself alone struggling and had no way of getting a nurse's attention. I understood the nurses in intensive care had many sick patients to care for. I happened to be a patient who had no ability to communicate or move my arm to ring for help. The longer I waited for help the more my body seemed to let go. I finally had to surrender to my body's normal function. I laid there motionless with my hands by my side feeling hopeless and finally surrendered my life that this might be the end. If my therapist hadn't walked into the ICU on his day off to check on me I wouldn't be writing this story today. It's certain that mankind cannot live without oxygen. What a web the Lord was weaving to capture my heart. ♥

Until you understand what you have been saved from you never fully appreciate the person who reached out to share the Gospel message with you. I had been to two churches growing up and had never considered Jesus in a personal way until a gentleman name Mr. Skidmore walked into my life one day and began to share his love for the Lord with my mom and me. We had never met this man before who had once suffered with the same disease. He took it upon himself to visit and was relentless in finding ways to share his healing experience with me.

Towards the last month of my hospitalization Mr. Skidmore brought a book to me titled, "Beyond Yourself" by Peter Marshall. Having finished the book I realized that I needed to make a decision for Christ. That decision only held until I found myself walking in a direction that God never would have approved of. I will always be grateful for Mr. Skidmore and for the Lord loving me enough to send someone to share Christ with me. ♥ When Jesus said that those that the Father has given Him no man can snatch away it's completely true. I made that faith statement in the hospital and though I went on to live a godless life for years Jesus remained my Savior until I made Him Lord.

Seven of the most powerful words were spoken to me one evening while having dinner with a friend. You have heard this story before, but this is where my personal journey with the Lord really began. I had just spent the last several years living a life that involved excessive drinking and immoral relationships and had recently been released from a ten day stay in a lockdown ward. While having dinner one night with the doctor who helped me through the days I was locked up, he looked at me from across the table and said, *"Do you know God can forgive you?"* Those seven words transformed my life and led me on a new journey. A journey that won't end until I take my last breath here on earth and my first in Heaven

19

He's Calling Your Name

MY JOURNEY INTO THE ARMS of the Father detailed many heart breaking roads I traveled in my lifetime. Since I truly believe in the verity of scripture, I must share with you what I wasn't aware of while growing up as a child and didn't consider before I began to write this book. Until I was able to see myself through the eyes of my Heavenly Father I had many questions I felt I needed answers to.

If I was known in eternity and brought forth by the loving hand of my Father as is written in the scriptures then I must ask myself; where was the Father when I was growing up? Did His presence in my life cease to exist the moment I was born? If so, did He hide Himself from all the unpleasant and painful things I suffered and experienced as a child? Where was God when help was needed to stop destructive events that took place in my life that should never happen to any child?

Throughout the Bible we see God as someone who is All-Powerful, All Knowing and an Ever Present God. If this is true, why did He not prevent what was happening to me if He had the power to do so? If I allowed myself to revisit my childhood it would lead me to cry out to God as David did in the Psalms when he said, "Why do you stand afar off O Lord? Why do you hide in times of trouble?" Like many of us, David had many questions that he felt he needed answers to.

I believe my questions were valid and would have loved the answers to them at one time. My past made it difficult for me to understand why no one seemed to step in and stop hurtful situations. Whether one claims to be a Christian or not, the truth we must realize is this, until the eyes of our understanding are opened we will continue to blame God for what we don't understand. I'm thankful I no longer struggle with the need to have answers. What happened to me was not something God ignored or allowed. He was very much aware of what I experienced.

When man is living with an unredeemed nature he does what his flesh desires for him to do. We cannot cast aside that each of us are given a freewill to choose how we live and the decisions we make each day. My birth father and my stepfather were both acting out of what their carnal nature demanded. Until my stepfather turned his life over to the Lord he continued to be controlled by his flesh. I understand all too well how our sin nature finds ways to allow the flesh to dictate the choices we make. I made many wrong choices without thought as to who I might be hurting in the process. Who do I blame and who should the people I hurt blame? Certainly not God! He gave me free choice and I abused it.

We live in an imperfect world that is full of all manner of evil. I find it heartbreaking to hear someone speak about the injustice they experienced and how they want to blame God. I hear these words all too often, "How can I believe in a God who allowed what took place in my life?" As I listen to their story my heart is overwhelmed with emotions that cause me to immediately want to respond with, "You have the wrong picture of who God is!"

The moment any of us pause long enough to visit our past with regards to the injustice we suffered we tend to blame God. I don't remember ever getting angry with God as a child for the way I was treated. I directed all my emotional resentment towards my stepfather. It's when I was older that I found myself at times saying, "Why me Lord?" I wasn't really blaming God as much as I wanted to understand what I had done wrong to feel so unloved at times.

It's only as I have grown to love the Lord and put my trust in Him and what He says regarding my life, that I'm able to leave many questions unanswered for a reason. Do I believe we will have all the answers to our whys? Not at all! What I am certain of is this; when I put my faith and trust in God regardless of what I'm unable to discern on my own, I experience His peace in my life. Allowing God to be sovereign over my circumstances shows that I am willing to relinquish my need to have all the answers.

Letting go will never be easy until our love and affection for the Lord is manifested in our lives. Regardless of how I interpreted events in the past or how I look at things in the future, He promised me this, "All things will work together for good to those who love God and who are called according to His purpose" Romans 8:28. Nurturing our love for God is such an important key to our letting go of what we don't understand.

Love becomes the building block for faith and trust to be fostered. Romans 8:28 is perhaps one of the most often quoted scriptures when experiencing uncertainties taking place in our lives. Many times we find ourselves with no forthcoming answers to what we are dealing with and this verse should encourage us to let go and trust God for the outcome He wants worked out in our lives.

Lauren Dagle sings a song that puts the trust issue in perspective. Her song "I Will Trust in You" sends a powerful message about our need to let go and have faith in the one who created us. When I find myself struggling and searching for answers the following words to her song rings in my heart. When You don't move the mountain I needed you to move. *When You don't part the water I wish I could walk through. When You don't give me answers when I cry out to You, I will trust in You. I will trust in You.* The words to this song will always challenge me to look at my situation with a different set of eyes when necessary.

It's so much easier to analyze our past or present situations in the natural because we are able to gather our information from what we feel, see and touch. This method of reasoning has proved to be destructive in my own life when I left out the element of trust. What I thought made sense with what I was experiencing wasn't what the Lord was doing in my life all.

It's easy to miss out on God's blessings when we lean on the arm of flesh rather than to trust what we are not able to see on our own. My wise husband once said to me, *"Hon, the more you try to figure out what is happening the less peace you're going to experience in life. You need to trust God because He knows what He's doing."* I may never understand why I had to experience certain events in my life that left scars. What I do know is this; my Heavenly Father brought me through each and every one of them and helped me heal through the power of His love.

The key to being able to trust and accept what we don't understand is discovering the depth of love the Father has for us. The purpose in writing my biography was to demonstrate the truth found in Ephesians 3:18, "May we be able to comprehend with all the saints what is the width, length, depth and height to know the love of Christ." The Father's desire for all His children is that we understand the magnitude of His love. If I have not shown the truth to these words by my story, then I have failed my assignment.

It's only as we establish our hearts in the Lord that we can begin to comprehend the full meaning of the above verse. I encourage you to stop here and reflect on the kind of love described in Ephesians 3:18. Think about how this verse may have applied to a particular situation in your past that the Lord was able to use to show you this depth of love. This chapter is meant to help us move from thinking we have an impersonal God to One who desires to be intimately involved in all aspect of our lives.

There is a vast difference between knowing about God and truly having experienced Him in your life. Experiencing God means that you have seen His very nature at work. Have you ever experienced His provision and known Him to be your provider? Have you experienced His healing power in your life when you cried out for healing for yourself or others? Have you felt His Spirit move in your life during the times you desperately needed someone to comfort you? This is the definition of experiential knowledge. When you see Him actively at work in areas like this you will see Him as a loving Father who cares about every aspect of your life.

There would have been no true depth to my time of intimacy with the Father if I limited my knowledge of who He truly is. Permit me to explain openly what would be the outcome of attempting to be intimate with the Father when you have so little knowledge or understanding of Him. Many of you can identify with the example I am about to share. When we chose to enter into a sexual relationship with someone we have just met or have not known for long, this cannot be considered an act of love. You are being intimate with one another out of your fleshly desires; however, real intimacy is developed as two people become acquainted with one another over a period of time. If I am to experience true intimacy in any relationship I must be willing to know the one I desire love from, not just the physical act of sex. Knowledge and experience are the two dynamics that will help us develop a belief in the Father's ability to love us.

When I struggled with my identity as to how the Father perceived me, I found it easier to believe what the world had to say regarding my life. It is only when I tried to imagine who the Father was by my own experiences that I distorted His true image. Overcoming years of negativity was never easy for me. Nevertheless, the Father's desire has always been for me to experience the magnitude of His love. Like so many of you, I allowed my childhood circumstances to create in me a barrier that prevented me from thinking it possible that I could ever be loved by the Heavenly Father.

My transition from knowing God to knowing Him as Father was not easy for me, but I never gave up seeking for my heart to accept His love. I am convinced that I have been asked to write this particular book to dispel the myth that God is someone who just sits on His throne waiting to judge us rather than embrace us. You can search the scriptures and you will not find that Jesus paints a picture of His Father as a God who is ready to pour out His wrath upon us. On the contrary! He is calling your name to come and take your place before His Throne. He created you for fellowship and communion with Him.

It is my hope that your journey will also lead you to find a home in the Father's embrace. May you experience what awaits those who surrender to His pursuit of them? Remember that each of you have a unique story of your own that is written by the hand of God. I cling to the scripture in Psalms 139:16 speaking about our Heavenly Father, "Your eyes saw my substance, being yet unformed, and in Your book they are all written, the days fashioned for me when as yet there were none of them." Such a personal Father He truly is.

His purpose and will for all of our lives was set in eternity. If you will take the time to reflect on what He has written in Psalms 139 concerning your life, you will know just how precious you are in your Father's eyes.

—20—
Pearl of Great Price

YOUR WORTH SHOULD NEVER BE MEASURED by the world's standards. It is only as we look to the cross we are able to see our true worth. There is no worthier description of how the Father places a value on our lives then what is found in Matthew's account of the Pearl of "Great Price." If we would choose to see our lives the way the Father sees them we would welcome His embrace without a moment's hesitation [Matthew 13:45-46].

You are the pearl the merchant was searching for. The Great Price that purchased your life took place at the cross. The brutality of what the Father allowed His Son to suffer served only one purpose. Through Christ's death mankind could be forgiven, and restored and have perfect fellowship with the Father. I hope you can see the Father's deepest desire is to have intimacy and communion with His people. Yes, you are the pearl of great price and let no one tell you differently!

Unfortunately, if you've been a Christian for any length of time you have encountered voices that tend to diminish your self-worth and hinder your relationship with the Father. I knew Jesus loved me but I also knew there was more. The relationship Jesus had with His Father was what I desired to have. I wanted to be the Father's daughter and Him to be my Father. I didn't know how to achieve that kind of relationship. I struggled with my identity and always saw myself unworthy to embrace it.

It wasn't only my inner voice that kept my heart from receiving God as my Father, it was the outside voices that often came from those I loved. There was a time even after being a Christian for years that I would still let voices try to redefine who I was. I knew once I exchanged my old life for a relationship with Christ it would probably take a lifetime for the rough edges of my life to change.

Sanctification is a lifelong process for any of us and it only happens when we submit ourselves to the Lord. When my unrefined personality offended someone unintentionally they often responded with hurtful words. I somehow interpreted their words as a sign that I wasn't loved. As childish as that may sound, there was too much of my background that prevented me from seeing it any differently. If they didn't love me how could the Father possible love me? Sad that the power of our words can be so damaging. It's true we receive in our lives what we sow in others. I'm ashamed to admit I haven't always been a sower of encouraging words but often times found my words to be insensitive when spoken.

Our human nature and inability to see others the way God sees them makes us unwilling to forgive the past. Scripture defines me the way I am viewed by the Father. People define me as to how I appear to them. I allowed the hurt and pain to affect me until I realized who I belonged to. That never became a reality until I was certain of the Father's love.

If we think back to our childhood we will remember how kids would say, "Stick and stones will break my bones but words will never hurt me." We may have believed that as a child but in all reality we know those words are far from the truth. Words at times are so powerful they set in motion something inside of us that causes us to respond either positively or negatively. When that happens we have to learn to recognize where the voice is coming from.

Our fight is not against those who project those negative words towards us. We are dealing with the real enemy of our lives. Flesh and blood represent who the enemy uses to accomplish his work in bringing us down. It's important to recognize the fight is not against people who choose to use the power of speech to express their dislike or disapproval of us.

We need to recognize that not all hurtful voices are meant to offend us. It is very important to discern which voices to listen to and which ones to reject. I realize that so much of my childhood played a tremendous role in how I viewed myself not only as a child but as an adult. I often felt sorry for myself and blamed my responses towards others on the way my home life was. It became an excuse for the way I was interpreting life. You can only play the blame game for so long until you wake up one day and realize you have felt sorry for yourself long enough.

I don't think I would have opened my eyes to this reality if it were not for someone who I loved and whom loved me enough to say, "*Janene, you need to stop using your past as an excuse for the way you feel.*" I felt hurt over anyone who came against me and would put my defenses up. If I was going to allow God to take some of the rough edges out of my life so that I wouldn't offend others, I had to hear what her voice had to say to me.

I didn't want my voice to be used to hurt others so I opened my heart up to listen to what she saw in my life. I invited her to spend one hour in my office and show me what I couldn't see in myself. That one hour experience was life changing. Her voice became a tool to encourage me to see things differently and avoid hurting others. We need to be willing to open our heart to the voice of love when it requires us to grow in areas of our life.

It would be wise to remove any doubt in our minds and heart that God may be some higher being ready to pour out His wrath upon us and who hides Himself from the unpleasant things we went through or may be facing. God was, is and always will be a loving Father who understands and cares about what you have faced in your life that has caused you pain. More people struggle with seeing God as a loving Father because their own father was either absent or abusive.

My life represented this solid brick wall that was created by the many situations that occurred not only in my childhood but also as a young adult. It took years for me to see the bricks removed, but that's exactly what happened. One brick at a time began to be taken down from the wall that held me in bondage. Though God is able and willing to do a quick work in our lives, often times the process is gradual and sometimes painful. Only the Lord with the help of the Holy Spirit can dismantle your personal wall that holds you back from enjoying true fellowship with the Father.

I love the illustration the Lord gave me when I was preparing this chapter and it has everything to do with John 15:16a. "You did not choose Me but I chose you." Most of us attended schools where during recess we were divided up into teams for different activities. Two kids were chosen to be the captains and each captain in turn began to choose the kids they wanted on their team. We waited in anticipation while hoping to be chosen first. Though I was not the last kid standing, I clearly identified with what was going through the heart of the ones who were picked at the very end. Those innocent games have a way of tearing down any self-esteem they may have felt about themselves. Thankfully it is not so with God! You were not chosen last, you are His first pick for any activity He has called and equipped you to do.

You have a distinct purpose that God ordained for you alone. The biggest challenge for us is to reach the place where we can agree with God when He says, "You are fearfully and wonderfully made" [Psalms 139:14]. He considers you the amazing work of His doing, and He wants you to believe that in such a way that you will never doubt His ability to love you again. Remind those who speak voices of condemnation that you are still a work in progress and let the negative words become powerless.

Each one of you are a true masterpiece designed and brought forth by the loving hands of your Father. David declared in Psalms 71:6 "By You I have been upheld from birth; You are He who took me out of my mother's womb." You were formed in eternity and made for eternity!

I once read a description of how the Father has your picture hanging on the walls of Heaven. You are not the clone of someone else but are truly unique all by yourself with a DNA that belongs to you alone. Every human, animal, flower, tree and every blade of grass has no DNA alike. Only you can be you. You were not the Father's afterthought. You were pre-determined in His heart before you were ever created.

I often think about these words to a song I remember from years ago. "To Know, Know, Know, Him, is to Love, Love, Love Him," I have applied these secular words to being the key to growing my faith and trust in the one who created me. Knowing who God is produces love and love in turn helps us to know with certainty who we are in the eyes of our Father. The experience the Father wants to have with you will be enriched when you understand and accept as truth how He sees you.

You are a Pearl of Great Price and no matter how long He must wait for you to surrender to His love, He will pursue you with open arms until that day.

♥ 21 ♥
A Reflection of
My Father's Love

I REMEMBER THE MORNINGS I would sit on the couch staring into the warmth of the fireplace glowing with flames that would take the morning chill away. I somehow felt mesmerized by the flames as they danced to a rhythm of their own. I felt warm and cozy as I held my Bible on my lap and spent time sharing my life with You.

I suddenly found myself lifting my eyes once again into the roaring flames and realized I was seeing a reflection of Your love for me. The flames no long presented a picture of warmth but seemed to echo a reminder to me of what I had been delivered from.

Hell was no longer my destiny where the fiery flames of Hell would continually burn with no way to escape from its penalty for my sin. Instead, You offered me forgiveness and a love I never knew existed.

Writing this book has opened my eyes to Your constant presence throughout my life. You had every right to condemn me to hell and yet, You were relentless in Your loving pursuit of me.

Today I am no longer fatherless. You are my Heavenly Father and I am Your Daughter.

Love Janene

In Closing

I OFTEN WONDER if I am to remain a writer sitting behind a desk never to stand before others to share my story. All I have ever wanted since being asked to be a writer for my Lord is to have the opportunity to show others the passion I have for the Father and the passion He has for me as His daughter.

Though I no longer struggle with believing in the Heavenly Father's love, I know many in the body of Christ do. I hear story after story of those who still feel the pain of their past childhood experiences. I pray that through the writing of this book there will be some who can finally believe in such an amazing love that our Heavenly Father has for them.

I am available should you have a church or group that may benefit from my testimony with the hope that it will bring healing to others in the areas that I struggled with.

Janene Prudler

Rechargeministries@gmail.com

520-508-4840

Made in the USA
San Bernardino, CA
09 August 2017